The Kingdom Economic Empowerment Seri

CW00495468

NO MORE DEBTS

Your broad guide to living above the World's Economic System and begin to Spend from God's Pocket.

Volume 1

By

Charles Omole

NO MORE DEBTS:

Published by:

WINNING FAITH
OUTREACH MINISTRIES

London . New York . Lagos

Isbn: 978-1-907095-00-9

CONTENTS

INTRODUCTION

"He that is faithful in that which is least is faithful also in much: and he that is unjust in the least is unjust also in much. If therefore ye have not been faithful in the unrighteous mammon, who will commit to your trust the true riches? And if ye have not been faithful in that which is another man's, who shall give you that which is your own?" (Luke 16:10-12.)

God is not **obligated** to make you **financially independent** if you are not willing to deal wisely with what He has given you - and be accountable. Accountable stewardship must, therefore, be the heart desire of every Believer who craves to experience financial independence.

Our **physical** and **material** prosperity depend to a large extent on our **spiritual** and **emotional** wellbeing. But even when we have developed a **prosperous mentality** (and know that God has empowered us to prosper), Satan would still try his best to cheat us out of God's will, if we are not **accountable** and **faithful** in our use of it.

Debt is not sin in the Bible. But all references to it in scriptures are from a negative viewpoint; hence we are supposed to avoid the burden it brings. We cannot live above a system if we are ignorant of its workings. Ignorance has led to many believers getting trapped by the Babylonian trivial gratification; which has led to many making a shipwreck of their faith and Godly testimony. So this book discusses a lot of the practical financial instruments and system employed by the Western economies to keep people under its control. We will also discuss solutions to demonstrate that you will always win by righteousness.

This book has been written as a study guide; hence some points have not been elaborated on, but merely stated. There are also a few one liners or short descriptions of some points. This is deliberate. I want this material to provoke further study and research in you. Also I have based most practical analysis on UK statues, so this will vary for other countries. Kindly note that this book is not a replacement for professional independent financial advise; which I will recommend you get, to implement some strategies from this material.

This book was written to help you understand and live a **financially prudent life** that glorifies and exalts JESUS CHRIST as LORD over your finances. Over the past ten years, I have thought at financial seminars with all manner of handbooks on financial matters. Some of these materials are included in this book for continuity. We need to be savvy about money as children of God.

I am advocating that you "spend" within your means and not "live" within your means. If we all live within our means as many believes; there will be no room for faith and promotion in matter of finance. So my intention is not to advocate poverty or restricted lifestyle. I merely wish that we become more informed and wise in matter of financial stewardship.

I am not advocating living small; even though it may seem like it in this book. I am only advocating living 'small' (spend within your means) as a way of getting out of the debt trap; so that you can go forth and live "Big" for God through righteousness. This is pure wisdom.

My prayer is that you would be transformed into a financial pillar in the Body of Christ as you read this book. And as you endeavour to apply the principles in it, you will not fail. You will succeed.

Welcome to the first day of the rest of your prosperous life.

It is well.
Charles Omole

BOOK OBJECTIVES

The objectives in this book are to help you:

1. **Develop a clear understanding of the will and purpose of God for your Finances.**
2. **Understand God's purpose for wealth and financial prosperity.**
3. **Learn the principles and attitudes that give birth to Accountability, Contentment and faithful Stewardship.**
4. **Understand the philosophy behind the world's Credit and Debit system.**
5. **Learn the importance of Budgeting and Giving.**
6. **Learn how to break the power of Debt over your life.**
7. **Develop the faith, discipline and maturity needed to be financially free.**
8. **Begin to spend from the Pocket of Jehovah.**

<u>Six</u> guiding principles are upheld throughout this book. They are:

1. **God is totally interested in the wellbeing of His people.** (Psalm 37:27b.)
2. **God always rewards faithful stewardship with quality.** (Luke 16:10–18.)
3. **Accountability honours God and becomes the bedrock for a Prosperous life.** (Luke 14:28-30.)

4. **Establishing God's Kingdom on the earth is the only godly basis for the Believer's Prosperity drive -** every other motivation is, at best, selfish. (Duet. 8:18.)

5. **Borrowing is not wrong, but it is to be avoided at all cost -** on our way to financial Independence. (Duet. 28:12)

6. **We cannot live above the system of this world if we are ignorant of it.**

1 Section

UNDERSTANDING THE FATHER'S WILL

THE FATHER'S HIGHEST WISH

"For the Lord God is a sun and a shield: the Lord will give grace and glory: no good thing will He withhold from them that walk uprightly." (Psalm 84:11.)

If there is one thing I have never ever doubted, it is that God wants every one of His children, who walk in the truth, to prosper in every area of life. The Apostle John echoed with pinpoint precision and divine accuracy the very mind of God, when his wrote:

"Beloved, I wish above all things that thou mayest prosper and be in health, even as thy soul prospereth." **(3 John 2.)**

It is therefore no surprise, that the very first thing God did to man after creating him was to **bless him** and **empower him to be fruitful**.

God has every reason to want his children to prosper. In fact, He is more eager to see us blessed in every area of life, than we can possibly imagine.

Here are **seven** reasons to prove it:

1. **God is your Father**
Do you know of any good father who does not want his children to make it in life, or who would not do everything in his power to provide for his children? God would be unrighteous to do any less for His blood bought children. (Matt. 6:31-32.)

2. **God loves you with an unconditional love.**
Anyone who lays down his life for you, must surely be willing to give you things of lesser value and importance. Well, all the riches of this world are nothing compared to the precious life of the Son of God, which was poured out for you on the cross. (John 3:16, Rom. 5:8.)

3. **God chose you to represent Him on the earth.**
You are God's Ambassador and you are a reflection of Him. If ungodly nations look after their diplomats, a completely righteous God will do no less for His. (2 Cor. 5:20.)

4. **God wants you to be able to give priority time to the work of the Kingdom**
That is usually not possible if you are struggling to make ends meet, when you are lumbered with three or four jobs, and when you've got more bills to pay than money to pay them with. (Matt. 6:33-34.)

5. **God wants you to be a blessing to others.**
When God called and blessed Abraham, He said He was calling him to be a 'Blessing'. You too have been called to bless others. But you can't do that effectively if you are in debt. (Matt. 5:13-14, Deut. 15:6-9..)

6. **God is in a Covenant with you.**
Covenants are entered into for mutual benefits. He created and owns everything there is; we've been cheated and impoverished by Satan our enemy. The good news is that our Covenant relationship with God tips the balance in our favour. Never stop thanking God for your Covenant of Restoration and Increase! (Psalm 89:34.)

7. **Blessing and prospering you would give God great pleasure.**
God is delighted when his kids are doing well. He is also sad when Satan cheats us out of what He has supplied for us. (Psalm 35:27b.)

CONCLUSION
There should be no doubt in your heart that the life God has called you to, is a prosperous and a healthy one.

GOD'S NUMBER ONE REASON FOR BLESSING US.

"For this is good and acceptable in the sight of God our Saviour; who will have all men to be saved, and come unto the knowledge of truth." (1 Tim. 2:3-4.)

We serve a God of purpose, who does everything for a special reason. We know from His word that He has already blessed us and wants us to stay blessed. Therefore, He must have a reason for doing so. Deuteronomy 8:18 makes this clear;

"But thou shalt remember the LORD thy God: for it is he that giveth thee power to get wealth, that he may establish his covenant…."

Therefore,

1. RECOGNISE THAT PEOPLE ARE PRECIOUS TO GOD
   - That's why Jesus Christ paid the ultimate price.

2. GOD'S COVENANT WITH US IS CENTERED AROUND BRINGING HIS LOVE AND SALVATION TO PEOPLE.
   - God fully intends to reap a global harvest (of souls) before his Son returns.

3. THE FATHER'S GAME PLAN FOR THE SALVATION OF MEN:

   i. **INTERCESSION**: Inspired Intercession for the Nations and people of the world.

   ii. **MOBILIZATION**: Commissioning and releasing missionaries to preach and demonstrate the full gospel message.

   iii. **FINANCING**: Strategic and systematic sponsoring of the Gospel into every corner of the earth.

4. INTERCESSION, PREACHING AND FINANCING THE GOSPEL ARE THE RESPONSIBILITIES OF EVERY CHRISTIAN.
    - However, the level of your participation in any area will depend on your inclination, gifts or calling.

5. EVERY CHRISTIAN SHOULD BE INVOLVED IN FINANCING THE GOSPEL THROUGH PRUDENT STEWARDSHIP AND FOCUSED FINANCIAL VISION.

   "But if any provide not for his own, and specially for those of his own house, he hath denied the faith, and is worse than an infidel." (Tim. 5:8.)

6. IF GOD HAS GIVEN YOU THE RESPONSILBILTY OF FINANCING THE GOSPEL, HE MUST HAVE MADE PROVISION FOR YOU TO DO SO ADEQUATELY AND EFFECTIVELY.

   - If He has not given you the responsibility of doing so, you are either a candidate for faithful intercession or a candidate to be sent – or both.

2

Section

HOW TO DEVELOP FINANCIAL ACCOUNTABILITY

SEVEN FOUNDATIONAL PRINCIPLES THAT LEAD TO A FINANCIALLY SECURE AND GENEROUS LIFESTYLE.

God showed me seven things that can open the door for Satan to cheat you out of your material blessings. They are a lack of understanding and practice of:

1. **THE PRINCIPLE OF STEWARDSHIP.**

   This principle teaches that you are first and foremost a steward of everything you have. God has put everything you own into your hands, and commands you to take good care of them. He is therefore entitled to make demands on them as He sees fit. This principle advocates that you be faithful.

   "And the Lord said, Who then is that faithful and wise steward, whom his lord shall make ruler over his household, to give them their portion of meat in due season? Blessed is that servant, whom his lord when he cometh shall find so doing. Of a truth I say unto you, that he will make him ruler over all that he hath." (Luke 12:42-44.)

2. **THE PRINCIPLE OF FAITHFULNESS – IN LITTLE THINGS FIRST.**

This principle teaches that the faithfulness (accountability) in the little things, qualifies you for 'bigger' and 'better' things in the eyes of God. It also helps you understand that being faithful in another man's business qualifies you for your own.

"He that is faithful in that which is least is faithful also in much: and he that is unjust in the least unjust also in much. If therefore ye have not been faithful in the unrighteous mammon, who will commit to your trust the true riches? And if ye have not been faithful in that which is another man's, who shall give you that which you own?" (Luke 16:10-12.)

3. **THE PRINCIPLE OF CONTENTMENT.**

This principle teaches you to make what you have and who you are in Christ, the basis of your contentment. When the All-Sufficient One is the source of your satisfaction, 'things' would literally pursue and overtake you.

"...for I have learned, in whatsoever state I am, therewith to be content." (Phil. 4:11.)

"...But godliness with contentment is great gain."

4. **THE PRINCIPLE OF PATIENCE.**

This principle teaches you exercise patience as you wait for the manifestation of your dreams, knowing that God has a 'perfect timing' and that waiting is part of maturing.

"But let patience have her perfect work, that ye may be perfect and entire, wanting nothing." (Jam. 1:4.)

5. **THE PRINCIPLE OF OBEDIENCE.**

This principle teaches you to be willing to do whatever God instructs you to do, and to do it with all your heart – knowing that your obedience qualifies you for 'the good of the land'.

If ye be willing and obedient, ye shall eat the good of the land..." (Isa. 1:19.)

6. **THE PRINCIPLE OF SOWING AND REAPING.**

This principle teaches you to sow continuously and wisely; and to anticipate a continuous harvest – just like the farmer does. You learn how to plant your spiritual or material seed, how to cultivate it, and how to stand firm until your harvest comes.

"But this I say, He which soweth sparingly shall reap also sparingly; and he which soweth bountifully shall reap also bountifully. Every man according as he purposeth in his heart, so let him give; not grudgingly, or of necessity: for God loveth a cheerful giver." (2 Cor. 9:6-7.)

7. **THE PRINCIPLE OF PRIORITISED DESIRES**

This principle teaches you to let your number one priority desire be the advancement of the Kingdom. When Kingdom needs are high on your agenda, God obligates Himself to supply and meet all your needs.

"But seek ye first the kingdom of God, and his righteousness; and all these things shall be added unto you." (Matt. 6:33; Psa. 37:4; Matt. 5:6; Mark 11:24.)

MORE ABOUT STEWARDSHIP AND FAITHFULNESS

1. REALISE THAT YOU BELONG TO GOD TOTALLY.

    - Because he purchased you back for His pleasure.

2. REALISE THAT YOU ARE ESSENTIALLY A STEWARD OF GOD'S BLESSINGS.

    - Implying that everything you have is on loan to you, and that you will have to account for how you use them.

3. REALISE THAT FAITHFULNESS IN 'LITTLE' THINGS IS WHAT QUALIFIES YOU FOR 'BIGGER' THINGS.

   - Implying that divine increase is a product of tenacity and faithfulness.

4. RECOGNISE THE VALUE OF EVERYTHING GOD HAS PUT IN YOUR CARE.

   - The value of a thing is set by the value and respect given to the one who owns it.

5. UNDERSTAND GOD'S PURPOSE FOR BLESSING YOU.

   - To give you the opportunity to work with Him
   - To increase and promote you.
   - To make you a Blessing to your generation.

6. LEARN TO ALWAYS PUT THINGS IN THEIR RIGHTFUL PLACE.

   - Never put 'things' before people.
   - Always be willing to release them back to God.

7. DEVELOP PATIENCE AND CONTENTMENT; STARVE SELF-CENTRED INDULGENCE.

   - We are to seek first the good of the Kingdom and others.

CONCLUSION:

Make a decision to do these things (with God's help) from today, and you will have no problem being accountable.

Worksheet 1

INSIGHTS INTO OUR FINANCIAL RESPONSIBILITIES

Read the following statements and **decide** on their accuracy or otherwise. **Write down what they mean to you.**

1. FINANCING THE GOSPEL & HELPLING PEOPLE IS THE **RESPONSIBILITY** OF EVERY CHRISTIAN. THEREFORE, IT IS MY RESPONSIBILITY TOO.
   *(1Tim. 5:8; Deut. 8:18.) **(True __ False __)**

2. YOU CANNOT FULFIL ANY OF YOUR RESPONSIBILITES EFFECTIVELY IF YOU ARE IMPOVERISHED OR CONSTANTLY IN DEBT.
   *(Matt. 15:14b; Matt. 7:4.) **(True __ False __)**

   Q. Some people say that God may not want them to have more than they need. How true is this concept?

   ____

3. THE ALTERNATIVE TO A LIFESTYLE OF FINANCIAL **STRUGGLE** AND **POVERTY** IS A LIFE OF **FINANCIAL INDEPENDENCE** AND **GENEROUS GIVING**.
   *(2Cor. 8:9.) **(True __ False __)**

   Q. Is the **grace** of generosity and financial Independence available to every Christian? Is it available to you?

   ____

   ____

   Q. What could you **do** for the **Kingdom**, **the people you love** and **for yourself**, if you were financially buoyant?

   ____

Q. Is it worth pursing financial Independence, when there are more important spiritual things to pursue?

Q. Which of the seven principles shared in this section do you think you need to work on? How do you propose to do so in the next month or so?

3

Section

THE DIABOLICAL SIDE OF BORROWING

NOTHING JUST HAPPENS IN THE FINANCIAL ARENA

"The rich ruleth over the poor, and the borrower is servant to the lender." (Prov. 22:7.)

Multinational Corporations and lending institutions pay millions of pounds annually for the services of highly skilful and shrewd PR gurus, whose job descriptions all have one thing in common - to get you to hand over as much of your hard earned money as possible.

Many are trained to sweet - talk you into mortgaging your future by borrowing more than you can conveniently handle. It is therefore no surprise that there are literally hundreds of people all around us who are heavily in debt and into buying on credit.

The point I am trying to make is that nothing just happens in the financial arena for life. There is a definite mastermind behind the credit and lending empires of the world; and this diabolic mind is out to milk you dry – if it can.

Therefore, the only way to prevent this shrewd task-master from sapping the joy of living out of your life is to understand him and be wiser.

UNDERSTANDING THE NATURE OF DEBT.

The Chambers 20th Century Dictionary defines **debt** as a state of **obligation**, or **indebtedness**. To be obligated means to be 'bound to', 'constrained by' or 'locked into paying' something owed or promised.

This definition has three main implications:

1. **Debt binds you to your Creditor** – in a way that might compromise and inconvenience you. When you are obligated in this way you are left to the creditors 'mercy'.

2. **Debt empowers your creditor to rule over you.**
   And often his demands may clash with your loyalty to your Lord.

3. **Debt places you under a 'merciless' obligation.**
   Your Christian duty is to pay back whatever you owe or face the penalty. A godly conscience will not absolve you of your responsibility to pay what you owe.

WHAT THE BIBLE TEACHES ON BORROWING

(Read: - 2 Kings 4: 1-7.)

1. BORROWING IS NOT INTRINSICALLY WRONG.
   Why not?

   i. **Because the Believer is meant to lend. And God would not encourage his people to be party to evil.** (Deut. 15:6.)
   ii. **Because God has been known to ask His people to borrow.** (Exod. 3:21-22; 2Kings 4:3.)
   iii. **Because borrowing creates opportunities to help people, bear each other's burden and form lasting relationships.** (Gal. 6: 1-2.)

2. IF THERE IS SUCH A THING AS 'GODLY' BORROWING, IT WOULD HAVE ALL (OR MOST) OF THE FOLLOWING ATTRIBUTES.

   i. **Godly borrowing would be based on hearing from God -** ***not yielding to impulse or desires.***
   ii. **Godly borrowing would aim to meet godly targets and needs -** ***not greed.***
   iii. **Godly borrowing would increase effectiveness and joy -** ***not dampen it.***
   iv. **Godly borrowing enjoys miraculous repayments or debt cancellation benefits.**
   v. **Godly borrowing does not come with worldly sorrows.**

A DEFINITON OF NEED

Subjectively; a need can be whatever results in a reduction of your overall effectiveness when you don't have it, and increases your effectiveness and joy when you do.

TEN KEY REASONS WHY PEOPLE GET INTO DEBT.

1. IGNORANCE

If you have a poor understanding of the credit system, interest rate fluctuations and/or investment pit falls, you can easily get sucked into debt.

"My people are destroyed for the lack of knowledge: because thou hast rejected knowledge, I will also reject thee, that thou shalt be no priest to me: seeing thou hast forgotten the law of the God, I will also forget thy children." (Hosea 4:6.)

2. BAD BUDGETING - OR NONE AT ALL

Some people think that budgeting is not an act of faith. How wrong can they be? Budgeting is precisely what motivates you to exercise your faith; especially when you find out that your income can't really cover your expenditure.

"For which of you, intending to build tower, sitteth not down first, and counteth the cost, whether we have sufficient to finish it?" (Luke 14:28.)

3. BUYING ON IMPLUSE

When you go out, train yourself not to buy anything that you did not **plan** to buy before you left home. Having a principle like this gives you an opportunity to **evaluate** how great a need this thing is, and decide whether you can afford to buy it now and at the price it is going for. This is particularly useful when buying expensive items.

"Whether therefore ye eat, or drink, or whatsoever ye do, do all to the glory of God." (1 Cor. 10:31.)

4. SPENDING ON HOPE

This often happens to people who have no fixed salary. They base their spending on what they hope to make – which is sometimes unrealistic or misguided. 'Spending on Hope' usually disregards the **'law of seasons'**. (Explained in # 10.)

5. PEER PRESSURE

If you buy things to keep up appearances or to keep up with the Jones'; you are being led by peer pressure not by the Spirit of God.

6. IMPATIENCE

There is a time for everything under heaven. That means that there is a **right** and a **wrong** time to do things. Waiting for the right time to purchase things is a virtue that many people don't know about. But it is crucial to the Believer who wants to stay out of debt.

7. MISMANAGEMENT OF FUNDS

If you meet someone who **spends recklessly** (eg. Buys a £5,000 powerful, Fun and game Computer set for his child) irrespective of whether they can afford it or not, you have met someone who does not understand **stewardship** and who **does not respect money.** Sooner or later, that person is going to run out of money.

8. DISOBEDIENCE

One advantage Christians have in the financial area is the privilege of asking God for **direction** before making a purchase. Some people either don't pray before buying because they don't really want God's opinion, or plainly disobey His promptings because they have their own agenda, either way, regret and debt are the results.

9. TEMPTATION AND LUST

Gambling is a good example of how the temptation to be rich instantly can cause people to waste their hard earned money.

10. SUDDEN REDUCTION OR LOSS OF INCOME

The **'Law of seasons'** is a spiritual law which declares that as long as the earth exists, things will **fluctuate** (Gen. 8:22.). That's why we have seedtime and harvest; cold and hot; summer and winter; times of plenty and times when we could do with more. The Believer who understands this **principle of life** would understand why saving is both an act of **Faith** and **Prudence.**

CONCLUSION

Debt is like a trap. It lures you towards the bait without warning you of the impending danger. Debt is cruel. It sucks at your self-esteem and leaves you exhausted. Avoid debt if you can!

"Owe no man any thing, but to love one another: for he that loveth another hath fulfilled the law." (Rom. 13:8.)

Worksheet 2

EFFECTS OF OVER-BORROWING

Large debts can have the following negative consequence on you. TRUE or FALSE? Discuss and explain your thoughts about them.

1. OVER-BORROWING WILL FRUSTRATE YOUR GOD-GIVEN VISION
   Q. How?

   ____

2. OVER-BORROWING WILL INCREASE AREAS OF SPIRITUAL WARFARE
   Q. In what ways?

   ____

3. OVER-BORROWING WILL OPEN DOORS OF ANXIETY, FEAR AND WORRY
   Q. Explain how this happens.

   ____

4. OVER-BORROWING CAN DISRUPT FAMILY LIFE/CAREER.
   Q. In what ways?

   ____

5. OVER-BORROWING WILL INCREASE THE DISTRACTIONS YOU FACE (Col. 3:1.)
   Q. In what ways?

   ____

6. OVER-BORROWING WILL SEEK TO CONSUME YOUR ENERGY AND CONTROL YOUR LIFE.
   Q. Explain how this can happen.

7. OVER-BORROWING WILL FRUSTRATE YOUR EFFORTS TO MAKE PROGRESS.
   Q. In what ways?

8. OVER-BORROWING WILL NEGATE OR PROLONG YOUR EFFORTS TO MAKE PROGRESS.
   Q. In what ways?

9. OVER-BORROWING WILL LIMIT YOUR FREEDOM.
   Q. How?

10. OVER-BORROWING WILL LIMIT YOUR ABILITY TO GIVE CHEERFULLY.
    Q. Explain how this can happen.

4 Section

RISING ABOVE THE CREDIT TRAP

INTRODUCTION

Over the last twenty years or so, our understanding of the scriptures have greatly increased. It is probably fair to say that the average Believer today has more knowledge of God's Word than he would have had only a few years ago.

We've come a long way from the days when Christians thought that they were destined to be poor, sick and uninvolved with this world's system – when the Salvation message was the only word you could expect to hear in a Church, and when very few people were bold enough to believe God for a better standard of living. Thank God, things have changed for the better in one respect. However, we must not be careless or overlook Satan's desire to corrupt and twist everything God has been doing in our lives.

Although he can't stop the spread of the Word of God, or turn back God's Restoration clock, he will continue to try to deceive, misinform, misguide and appeal to the lust of our carnal nature. However, we don't have to be roped in and deceived if we understand the dangers and the pitfalls of the credit system.

CREDIT IS NEITHER GOOD NOR BAD

In one sense it is true to say that using the credit system is neither good nor bad. It really depends on how you use it. However, what is frightening about the credit system is the diabolical mastermind behind it, that seek to exploit people's ignorance and impatience. Please note that the word debt in this section and in the entire book refers to personal debt rather than business debt. This book is about personal finance and not business financial planning.

In other words, Credit can initiate a lot of positive things in your life when you take advantage of it wisely; and on the other hand, this modern financially 'convenient' system can bring untold misery to you if 'it' takes hold of you.

If you are a Christian, you have a distinct advantage in this respect. **You can take advantage of the credit system because you have a reservoir of information, wisdom and discipline to excel in these matters.** But merely having these qualities residing in you is not enough. You must KNOW them experientially and be yielded enough to God to follow His leading. You must also want to be financially free.

UNDERSTANDING THE CREDIT SYSTEM

METHODS OF PURCHASING.

There are generally three ways of purchasing things nowadays:

1. CASH: Money in coins and notes
2. CHEQUE: A written order to a bank to pay out money from your account.
3. CREDIT SYSTEM: A system of doing business which entrusts you to pay at a later date.

THE PSYCHOLOGY OF PURCHASING.

1. CASH REPRESENTS **PAST** HARD WORK, TIME, PAIN, SWEAT.

   So when you purchase with cash, you will tend to spend less, because all your emotions are involved in releasing that money.

2. A CHEQUE REPRESENTS **PRESENT** SPENDING POWER, A LIFELESS FIGURE ON A PIECE OF PAPER OR A COMPUTER SCREEN.

   When you purchase with a cheque, less of your emotions are involved. You are only limited by your account balance or overdraft facility. Therefore, you would tend to spend more than you would if you paid by cash.

3. CREDIT REPRESENT **FUTURE** INCOME, SALARY PAID AFTER THAT PROMOTION, MONEY MADE ON THAT CHERISHED ULTIMATE JOB, PROFIT CLINCHED WHEN YOUR BUSINESS IS ESTABLISHED.

   When you purchase on credit, you are tempted to move into the fantasy realm of high rollers. There is no connection between you and the commitment you are making. In addition to being emotionally detached from credit, 'low payment plans' are waved at you to give you the impression that you are getting a good deal. **You will always spend much more than you planned to spend when you buy on credit.** This is appropriately called **'Mortgaging your future'.**

CONCLUSION

1. If you want to spend less, pay with cash.
2. Most Salesmen are trained to entice you with credit. That way you spend more and everyone – but you - benefits.
3. Low payment plans are always **high** in the end.

POSITIVE AND NEGATIVE CREDIT

'Credit' was somebody's idea to help you get now, what you can't afford now. This can either be positive or negative.

Credit is *positive* if you:

1. Enriches or profits you
2. Empowers you to be generous
3. It Reduces time wasted
4. It Saves you money, and

5. It Reduces stress and anxiety

Credit can be *negative* if it:

1. Doesn't improve your overall position
2. Makes you greedy and tight-fisted
3. Costs you an arm and a leg
4. Increases your stress level
5. Hinders faith and fuels impatience

UNDERSTANDING LOANS

A loan is neither **good** nor **bad**: it depends on why you take it and what you do with it. But most references to borrowing in the Bible are negative; hence it should not be your preferred cause of action. But as it is impossible to put God in a strait jacket; it is not possible to say God opposes every borrowing. Investment or Business borrowing for instance is permissible if certain criteria are met.
"For the LORD thy God blesseth thee, as he promised thee: and thou shalt lend unto many nations, thou shalt not borrow; and thou shalt reign over many nations, but they shall not reign over thee" (Deut. 15:6.)

I have no problem with a LOAN – when necessary. What I want to warn you about is GREED. And there is a fine line of distinction.

Taking a loan can be a OK when we:

1. **Ascertain God's approval.**
   He approved one for the children of Israel just before they left Egypt. This loan made them wealthy to start with, and then because they forsook God, it became the basis for their down fall.

2. **Exercise due restraint.**
   There used to be a time when your Bank Manager genuinely had your best interest at heart. When he wanted to retain your custom for mutual benefit, and because his success at doing that was an indication of his effectiveness. However, things have changed. The 'god of this world' has tightened up his belt and is using the weapon of **debt** to destroy unsuspecting people. That's why the Christian must exercise great restraint.

3. **Examine all the alternatives.**
   There are always alternatives to going for a loan. They are not always better or easier on your ego, they may reduce stress or give God an opportunity to work a miracle for you. Examples of alternatives include: waiting until you can really afford it; Believing that God would supply it through others; choosing to go without: purchasing a less expensive one; etc.

4. **Are sensitive to Divine timing.**
   Divine timing, more often than not, speaks of ease. All things will work together for your good. Everything you do tends to produce peace in you. Divine connections seem to pop up just when you need them. And so on! When you are under pressure or when you feel confused, it is almost certain that the timing is wrong – all things being equal.

5 Section

DEBT FREE FOR LIFE

HOLDING DEBT TO RANSOM

You would struggle with debt for most of your life if you have a **debt mentality.** A person with a debt mentality, is one who has believed the lies of the enemy that say, "You must borrow if you want to buy anything of value", "you must make mortgage payments for the rest of your life (25 years or more)" or "You can only enjoy your life if you live on credit".

But there is a better way to live. There is a brighter future for every Christian who loves God enough to follow His recipe.

To start out, **renew** your mind to the following truths:

1. **No condition is permanent when it is committed to the Lord.**
   (Phil.4:6-7; Mark 11: 23; Cor. 4:17-18.)

2. **The "cattle upon a thousand hills" belong to your Daddy; and He is not stingy.**
   (Psalm 50:10-15; Psalm 34: 8.)

3. **God will meet your needs according to His riches in glory, if you don't limit Him with disobedience and unbelief.**
   (Phil. 4:19; Isa. 1:19-20.)

4. **God has great pleasure in the prosperity of His people.**
   (Psalm 37:4-5; Psalm 35: 27b.)

5. **God's financial plan for you does not depend on the world's system or on your past record - only on your faith for it, and God's faithfulness to keep His promise.**
   Mark 11:23-24; Psalm 29: 34.)

GEARING UP TO WIN YOUR FINANCIAL BATTLES.

If you have a debt problem, you did not get into it overnight; so it would probably take you some time to get out of it. **But the feeling of freedom is always worth the temporary inconvenience you may experience.**

Therefore, you must have a plan to get out of it. You can also expect a struggle to start with, because:

- i. **The financial god of this world does not want to lose your custom.**
- ii. **Your flesh does not want to give in to a life of discipline.**
- iii. **It takes time to destroy seeds sown and develop new habits.**

POSITIVE ACTION PLAN

1. **Renew your mind to the will of the Father.**
   Read passages like: Deut. 15:6; 3 John 2; Deut. 28:1-14; 2 Cor. 8:9; Rev. 5:9-10; Psalm 37:3-5, 23-26; Eph. 1:3 and 1 John 5:4-5.

2. **Prayerfully develop a plan to get out of debt. (2 Cor. 10:3-6.)**
   Both spiritual and positive action is needed, if you want to see things change quickly. Possible strategies include:

i. Paying much more than you planned to pay, if you can afford it.
ii. Consolidating all debts into one, and going for the most reasonable lender.
iii. Selling any redundant luxuries to improve cash flow.
iv. Putting extra money into clearing all the short term loans first.
v. Cutting down on non-essential stuff.
vi. Believing God for a raise, promotion or better job - and ploughing all funds into getting out of debt.
vii. Doing something with your talents, gifts and abilities (for habitually lazy Christians)

3. **Honour God by tithing on your income - even if that hurts like mad.**
(Prov. 3:9-10, Malachi 3:10-12.)
When you are hard off, one of the first things you are tempted to axe is your giving. Don't! When you stay faithful in your giving to God, you are symbolically saying that you trust, honour and respect Him more than your problems.

4. **Prove God's Word by blessing someone however you can.**
You may not have money to give, but you may be able to give up some of your time, or help someone achieve their goals. Whatever you do for someone else (to honour God), he will cause men to do for you much more. (Luke 6:38.)

5. **Plan what you will do when you are out of debt.**
Examples:
i. Organise a 'get-together' to share your testimony and victory.
ii. Support a couple of helpful ministries.
iii. Teach others how to become free from debt.
iv. Help some members of your family financially.
v. Get your spouse that long overdue gift.
vi. Go to Bible School.

Notes

6 Section

How to Get Out Of Debt - *Practical Concepts*

1. Why We Get Into Debt

Most of us have phases where we spend money like water. It could just as easily be a good or bad week at work, your best friend getting married, or a new baby in the family -- that sets you off on the slippery slope towards further destitution. And it's often not until a month later, when the dreaded statement for your credit or store card drops on the mat, that the consequences of your spending spree hits home.

Actually, sometimes it doesn't even hit home -- particularly if you don't open the statements! And by then, of course, three pairs of brand new designer shoes have been consigned to the back of the cupboard because they pinch. Or you've decided you don't like that CD after all, or that £500 suit. And you can't face the hassle of taking your purchases back to the shop!

But what happens if you lose your job? Get made redundant? Or get fired? It's that awful moment when you suddenly realise the true meaning of 'up the creek without a paddle'! Perhaps you don't even think you're actually 'in debt' anyway. Well, if you've got a loan of any kind, then you are! And the interest you are paying on those debts is money you've slogged your guts out to earn. It should be in your pocket, not that of a lender, don't you think? If things seem pretty bad at the moment, here are three reasons to be cheerful:

- Don't panic! You can't go to prison for being in debt (with some exceptions -- Crown debts in the UK for instance -- but we needn't go into this here).
- Take control of the situation. OK, you've got yourself into debt, but it's not the end of the world. You're not the only one and you're not a leper! You've

just miscalculated, that's all. The minute that you start taking responsibility again, you will start feeling better. Honest!

- If seriously in debt, then contact your creditors before they contact you. Believe it or not, they do not want to take court action unless it is absolutely necessary. But the problem will not only remain if you ignore them – it will most definitely get worse. Nothing annoys a creditor more than someone ducking and diving. If you know that you are getting into difficulties, talk to your creditors.

Don't ever forget that, in spite of the obstacles that constantly surface to make life just that bit more bloody difficult, money is not your Master. It is your Servant! If you can truly take on board that fact - and it IS a fact -- you will suddenly discover that you are the 'controller' and not the 'controlled'.

Remember that people get into debt for a number of reasons. While there are some who have lots of money and are truly irresponsible with it -- Spend, Spend, Spend whenever they can - the main causes are often more the result of bog-standard things like a relationship break-down, the loss of a job, or a business going down the pan. The ensuing depression that sometimes accompanies such a dramatic change in circumstances can make it even more difficult to summon up the will or the energy to deal with it.

The ploy is to face these things head-on and devise a method of dealing with them. Be the Master. Don't ignore the problem. The longer you delay, the longer it will take to sort out -- and the harder it will be to deal with.

2. How Much Do Your Debts Cost You?

You may owe vast amounts of money to various people, or perhaps just a teeny weeny bit -- but, whatever the size, you are bound to be paying interest on it. Just about everyone charges interest on what they lend you and, occasionally, we need reminding about what 'interest' actually is.

I dare you to take a £10 note out of your pocket and set fire to it! Watch it burn. And then do it to another £10 note. You didn't do it, did you? Of course that is a bad idea. I'm not surprised. The idea of watching 'real' money disappear, never to be seen again, is a tad disturbing. But it's what you're doing every time you only pay off the minimum on your credit or store card -- or whenever you make that monthly payment on your car loan. Part of your payment consists of the ashes of that £10 note.

Am I beginning to get the point across? There's no difference between burning a £10 note and not seeking out the best price. Well, there is -- one requires direct action, the other only requires you to sit on your backside. And, if you do the latter, you'll just be burning up all those £10 notes and will get a reputation for being one of the best customers of all those financial institutions out there! In other words, a sucker!

If you look after the pennies, the pounds will look after themselves, and it's time to finally take that old proverb on board -- even if your mother has been spouting it at you ever since you were in primary school!

While you almost certainly know what the interest rate is -- and while you know how much your repayments are each month -- do you really know how much you will be paying overall?

It's far too easy to borrow -- by sticking something on the credit card -- and it's far too easy to not pay it off each month. Be careful. Be realistic! One thing you can do is to realise that by removing your debt you **ARE**, in fact investing. If the APR on your credit card is 10%, for example, you are getting a 10% p.a. return on any amount by which you reduce the outstanding balance. So, you are not just improving your position by the amount of reduction, but by that extra 10% as well! What's more, this fabulous rate of return is guaranteed, no matter what the share market does!

By all means, keep a very small sum for emergencies, but, otherwise, use your savings to pay off as much as possible. Every little helps, and the more effort you make now, the sooner you'll be sorted out and on the path to comparative riches

3. Assessing Your Debt Problem

The first step to getting out of debt is to ascertain just what your position is. There's a bit of a procedure here but it's easy to follow -- you just have to look at a list and fill in the boxes. It's a pain having to spend half an hour digging out the latest bank statements and bills so you've got the information to hand. But it's worth it. I promise!

Now, don't panic! The simple aim is to sort out what income you have, what your essential outgoings are and what the debts are. To be honest, it's pretty useful to see the full extent of the problem in black and white. You won't like it -- you might even be a bit shocked at how reckless you've been. Nevertheless, be brave, fill in the form and print it off. But, before you do, let's look at each aspect of what we're trying to achieve:

What's your income?

What we're looking for here is every scrap of income after tax that you actually have coming into the household. We all have an income of some sort, whether it's your/your partner's salary, maintenance payments, benefits or tax credits. If you have a lodger, don't forget to include the income from that. This forms your Total Net Monthly Income. Tot it all up and see what you've got.

What do you spend?

Next come the essential outgoings needed to keep body and soul together. We're not talking about the 'debts' as that is a separate issue. What we mean is the monthly mortgage/rent, gas, electricity and water rates, the council tax, the TV licence, telephone, house and car insurance, pension, basic groceries, etc. If you're behind with any of these, don't include the debt aspect.

It's important to remember that there is a big difference between Needs and Wants. A 50p loaf of bread to make sandwiches for work is a Need. Buying a ready-made sandwich for £3 because you can't be bothered to make it yourself is a Want. Over a period of just one month the latter option could cost you £50 extra.

What we're drawing up here is a list of the Needs for general day-to-day living over a period of a month -- in other words, your Essential Monthly Outgoings. Add it all up and see what it comes to.

What have you got left?

Using the two figures from above, deduct your essential outgoings from your monthly income and you will be left with the sum of money the Net Disposable Income -- that you can spare to tackle the debts. Have you got enough coming in each month to cover those essential bills, with a bit to spare? If not, don't worry -- we'll think of something later. If you have, then let's press on.

Debts

This is where you have to take a deep breath and make a list of the actual debts. These include credit cards, store cards, bank overdraft, car loans, any other loans, and any arrears from your list of essential monthly outgoings. It's best in cases where an interest rate is charged - and there usually is -- to state the rate of interest. That way you can see at a glance which debts are costing you the most.

4. Snowball Your Debts

When thinking about how to tackle your debts, you'll find you have a number of options to consider. These include getting a better deal on your credit card debts by transferring them to a low-interest rate card, consolidating the debts by getting a personal loan at the lowest possible interest rate, or even releasing some of the equity in your home by re-mortgaging. The aim in any or all of these options is to get a better deal so that you are freeing up as much money as possible to put towards paying off the debts. But all of the above carry health warnings as individual cases vary. So get expert advise.

If you're not in a position to do any of these things then it's time to prioritise. Can you meet at least the minimum payment for each debt? And do you have some money to spare to feed the most voracious debt, ie: the one charging the highest interest rate?

If so -- then do it! Throw as much as you can at the most expensive debt until it's cleared while making minimum payments on the others. Then tackle the next one, and the next one, and the next one!

One technique you could try is known as snowballing. The idea of snowballing is to single out one credit card as your target and throw all the money you can at it whilst making minimum payments on all the other debts. Once you've paid off your first target debt, you then use all that freed-up money to tackle the next one on your list.

From a psychological point of view, some people find it easier to tackle the smallest debts first -- regardless of how much they're actually costing in interest charges. This method does at least induce a sense of satisfaction more quickly -- and if it's the one that works for you -- then reassure yourself with the thought that at least you are doing something. However, bear in mind that it will take longer to clear your debts overall if the smallest ones also happen to be the cheapest to finance.

5. Dealing With Your Creditors

If your creditors are really on your back and you're refused either a consolidation loan or a cheaper credit card to handle your debts, then it's time to become even more pro-active.

Try to persuade the people to whom you owe money to give you a little leeway. Make a proposal to them based on your ability to pay, i.e. using the monthly surplus (or net disposable) income. The simplest way is to deduct, say, £50 to cover emergencies and then divide the surplus equally between all creditors.

Write to them all, enclosing a copy of your Statement of Affairs, and make an offer of payment. Point out that, while you intend to pay everybody in full eventually, you cannot give them what you don't have. Offer to review the position on a monthly/quarterly basis and tell them that, whenever possible, you'll increase the payments. Crucially, you ask if they will freeze any further interest charges in the meantime.

Don't expect the sort of response that says: "There, there, of course, Old Thing. Never mind -- everything's going to be fine." There is going to be a great wailing and a gnashing of teeth (in some cases)!

The credit controllers working for these companies are not concerned with the rest of the people you owe money to -- they are only interested in what you owe them! So it is likely that you will get a bit of huffing and puffing. Don't panic! It's their job.

So, if they start threatening court proceedings, politely write back to them and point out that you have made the only proposals that you are able to in the circumstances. State, very politely, that, in the event that they issue proceedings, you reserve the right to produce all correspondence for the attention of the Court. If you have shown good faith, then it is likely the Court will respect that and will order payment along the lines of what you originally proposed anyway. Credit card and finance companies know this -- they just count on you not knowing this!

Alternatively, you could also say that it is disappointing that they will not accept your offer and, unless they can make other suggestions, you will have no alternative but to consider making an application for an Individual Voluntary Arrangement (more on this later) or even bankruptcy. This often has the "I've just lost the contents of my bowel" effect and, in most cases, they will see sense.

Unfortunately, there are no guarantees. So, what if they sue you? Then they sue! By this time, your credit rating will have collapsed anyway. So when you receive the summons, simply make the same offer of payment -- and there is a section on the summons form to do this -- and return it to the Court.

6. The Dos And Don'ts Of Ditching Debts

If you are really serious about getting yourself financially straight, it is vitally important that you abandon all thoughts for the time being of taking a holiday, getting a better car or replacing your temperamental VCR or DVD player. Many people roll out this sort of excuse: "I've got huge debts of £30,000 -- so another £500 won't matter! And besides, I really need a holiday because I've been worrying so much recently!"

But you need to grasp the fact that you could be risking the roof over your heads for the sake of a short-term happiness fix. It's understandable to want to get away from it all when everything is crowding in. And, if you're the sort of person who does this kind of thing, we're not going to beat you around the head with a cricket bat. We're just trying to make you screech to a sudden stop and *think!*

If you're honest with yourself, you'll probably realise you're in a bit of a mess right now because the costly fun things took priority instead of the essentials. It's far more satisfying to pay for something by yourself, instead of borrowing it from someone else at vast expense and then worrying about how to meet the bill. If you want the occasional treat to keep you going while clearing your debts, pick a small one such as a book or a CD. Don't forget that, when you were a child, small things gave you an immense amount of pleasure. They still can. You really don't *need* the expensive things.

7. Re-mortgaging and Getting Out Of Debt

Rising house prices have meant that many homeowners now have plenty of equity in their homes and one increasingly popular method of dealing with debts is to consolidate them by increasing your current mortgage or by taking out a separate home loan with another lender that is secured against the property.

This is not necessarily a good idea but it can work for some people if it's handled properly. You have to weigh up the pros and cons. By using your home as security for the loan you will almost certainly be able to borrow the money to pay off your debts as long as you have sufficient equity. And you are also quite likely to get a much more advantageous interest rate than you might have on all your standard credit card debts. If you have half a dozen different debts all with interest rates that are in double-digit numbers, then an interest rate of 5% or less can sound very attractive.

However, and this is probably the most important consideration when borrowing money against your house, you will be putting your home at risk if you can't meet the payments every month. If mortgage interest rates were to go up you might find you can't afford to make your monthly payments and your lender would have the right to re-possess your home.

You should also bear in mind that a loan secured against your home can last as long as your mortgage so you could end up paying much more overall. Your monthly payments may be lower because you've shifted your various debts to just one debt against the house but it's likely to be spread over a much longer term. So, if you ever borrow extra money this way then try and keep the term of the loan as short as possible. If you opt for increasing your current mortgage, for example, then ensure that you can overpay in order to reduce the debt more quickly.

You may find that if you switch your entire mortgage to a different lender that you can borrow more money to pay off your other debts without increasing your monthly payments at all. Most of the best deals on offer are for new customers and, by moving your mortgage to a new lender you will become a new customer.
There are plenty of financially savvy people who do this on a regular basis, even without borrowing more money, just to take advantage of the best rates. But if you do this, there are a number of things you need to consider.

For a start you may have redemption penalties to take into account. These could be sizeable and may well offset the savings you gain by refinancing in the first place. Then there are likely to be legal fees which could cost you roughly £300 and £500. Your new lender will probably also charge an arrangement fee for setting up the mortgage and you can bet your bottom dollar they'll want a survey done on your home too. Arrangement fees can cost around £250 and surveys anything from £200 to £500 for the average house.

Nevertheless, the savings could still be substantial not least because some lenders may offer to pay some or all of these fees as a way of enticing you to switch to them. The larger your current mortgage, the more you are likely to save and these savings could be put towards your debts - perhaps without even having to increase your mortgage.

Alternatively you could phone your current lender and threaten to switch to someone else. If you've had your mortgage with them for a while and are considered a valued customer they may well offer you a better deal just to keep you. Using your home as collateral for borrowing more money - especially if it is just to consolidate your debts - can be risky. So make sure you've thought it through properly. However be careful not to push too hard, as things are a bit tight in the market at the moment given the current economic climate. Above all, if you use a home loan to pay off your collection of debts, remember you've only converted them all into one large debt and that it still needs to be paid off. And, that, this time, you've borrowed against the roof over your head.

8. The Dangers Of Debt Consolidation

If you're trying to sort out a debt problem then you need to know exactly what those debts are. You can do this using a Statement of Affairs calculator. You may well find that you've got debts littered all over the shop. If you owe money for a car loan, an overdraft, a couple of credit cards and a store card, that's five separate debts. No wonder it's been hard work keeping track of your spending.

One option is to consolidate all the debts by borrowing a lump sum to pay off all the individual debts, so that you've only got one payment to make each month. Be warned that such loans are only a good thing if you actually use them to see off your creditors -- without incurring any further debts! Getting a consolidation loan only means you have amalgamated your debts, you haven't actually *cleared* them, despite what the TV adverts might have you believe.

It's estimated that about 80% of people who take out a consolidation loan go on to run up further debts. Of course, you want to be one of the other 20%! Your credit card statements will tell you that you no longer owe anything and it'll be very tempting to dip into your available limit. Don't! Be determined, be frugal, be sensible. And don't be one of those people who incurs further debt by not heeding this very important rule. A consolidation loan may well help you manage your money better but until it's paid off, you won't be out of the woods.

There are a number of things to look out for when looking for a consolidation loan. The interest rate is obviously the most important -- it should be the lowest you can find. But don't borrow more than you need. Many lenders will offer lower rates if you borrow more but don't fall into that trap. You might think it would be good to have a nice holiday after getting all those different creditors off your back but remember you will still have to pay it back -- and with interest too.

If possible it should also be flexible so that you can pay off more than the required amount if you suddenly find you can afford to increase the repayments. Many loans incur penalties if you pay them off early -- and quite a lot of people do -- so a flexible loan is best.

Your lender will probably try to persuade you take out payment protection insurance. Again, think hard about whether you really want it as it will add a considerable amount to your loan. The insurance is to protect them should you find yourself made redundant or ill and unable to work and it often doesn't kick in for a couple of months anyway. It's up to you to decide whether that misfortune is possible or likely but usually these policies are pretty expensive and a waste of money. You may prefer to pay for what insurers like to describe as 'peace of mind' but just remember that it's their peace of mind you're paying for!

Also, try to spread the loan repayments over as short a period as possible. The longer you take to pay off your loan, the more you'll pay in interest and the less motivated you will be to stay out of further debt. The important thing is to make sure that you can comfortably make the payments.

And finally, shop around. Don't be tempted by many of those dreadful adverts for loans that get shown on afternoon telly -- unless you want a high interest, inflexible loan that is secured against your home. A consolidation loan is a long-term commitment so make sure you choose it as carefully as you might choose a spouse!

9. IVAs and Bankruptcy (Based on UK Statutes)

In some cases, your debts might be so great that you have no hope of paying them off. However, it's not the end of the world as you still have two final options: an Individual Voluntary Arrangement (IVA) and bankruptcy.

Recent changes in bankruptcy law, plus the increased levels of debt many of us have taken on, has led to a massive increase in the number of people taking these routes, as the table below shows:

Year	Bankruptcy	IVAs	Combined
1997	19,892	4,549	24,441
1998	19,647	4,902	24,549
1999	21,611	7,195	28,806
2000	21,550	7,978	29,528

Year	Bankruptcy	IVAs	Combined
2001	23,477	6,298	29,775
2002	24,292	6,295	30,587
2003	28,021	7,583	35,604
2004	35,898	10,752	46,650
2005	47,291	20,293	67,584
2006 (H1)	31,772	18,889	50,661

Source: The Insolvency Service

Individual Voluntary Arrangement

An Individual Voluntary Arrangement (IVA) is a way of going bankrupt without actually going the whole hog. Essentially, you come to an agreement with all your creditors about how to pay off the debts. It's done under the supervision of a licensed Insolvency Practitioner (usually an accountant or lawyer) who usually does all the work with you and for you and, once in place, it has the force of law.
The good thing about an IVA is that it stops your creditors from knocking at your door and it enables you to have a great deal more control over how your assets are dealt with than you would with bankruptcy. It also may affect your professional status, if you have one, and a note of the IVA will remain on your credit record for six years.

The bad thing is that it all costs money to implement -- and that's money that you could have used to pay off your debts. So you should certainly shop around for the cheapest offers when you're looking for an Insolvency Practitioner as fees vary considerably. Also note that, in the event that you default on making payments in accordance with the agreement, your Insolvency Practitioner is obliged to petition for your bankruptcy. So, if your debts are serious enough to go the IVA route, you need to follow it through properly!

An IVA usually lasts for between two and five years, depending on how long it takes you to pay off your creditors. You will be required to account for your spending and anytime you get a pay rise, the extra money has to go towards the debts. If you have equity in your home or an endowment policy then you may be required to use these to pay off part of your debts.

Your Insolvency Practitioner will help you to sort out what your assets and liabilities are, how much you need to live on and how you propose to deal with your creditors. He'll then help you to apply to the court for an Interim Order, which puts an immediate stop on creditors taking legal action against you. The Insolvency Practitioner then contacts all your creditors and outlines your payment proposals. This can either be done in writing or he can call a meeting of your creditors -- it depends entirely on the extent of your debts and the number of creditors involved.

Provided 75% (in value) of creditors agree to it (and they usually will since it means they'll at least get some money out of you) the IVA can then be implemented. The fees you pay to the Insolvency Practitioner are normally taken out of the monthly payment you make to your creditors.

Many people have concerns with the way IVAs are being promoted to those in debt, particularly by the new breed of IVA firms that advertise heavily on TV and in the press. As these firms generate large fees from IVAs, there is obviously an incentive for them to recommend this solution when it may not be in the debtor's best interest (people on benefits being one example).

Note that there are moves to make the IVA process simpler, especially for those people who owe less than £30,000. However, the current system will be with us for a little while yet. The Statutes in countries outside of the United Kingdom may be different, so check this out with your local authorities.

Bankruptcy (Based on UK Statutes)

It goes without saying that this is truly a very last resort! Bankruptcy is a very serious matter and the fact is, it's probably not going to be up to you anyway. Although you can petition for bankruptcy yourself, if you're in that much trouble, it's more likely to be one of your creditors who will take this course of action against you.

Incredible as it may seem, creditors who are owed as little as £750 can make you legally bankrupt. It's unlikely for such a comparatively small sum, but it's worth remembering that the threat is there. In practice, if your total debts are less than £5,000 then you can apply to the court for an Administration Order instead. The court will then assess your financial situation and order you to pay off your debts, usually by monthly instalments.

It depends on the extent of the debts, of course, but if you're made bankrupt, you will probably lose just about everything apart from your pension. An Official Receiver or

Insolvency Practitioner will be appointed to take over the management of your financial affairs. Effectively, it means he takes over everything you own and sells the lot to clear the debts.

If your debts exceed your assets, the only things you'll be allowed to keep will be some basic household items and any tools you need in order to work. If you have any income over and above what's necessary to live on, you will have to hand that over, too. And if you want to have a bank account, you have to tell them you're a bankrupt.

The good news is that, due to a recent change in the law, most bankrupts will now be automatically discharged after just one year and, in some cases, discharge could come even earlier. And although you are still liable for your debts for three years after being made bankrupt, after that the remaining debts are written off leaving the discharged bankrupt is free and clear to make a fresh start. Note however that you will still have to pay any student loans you took out.

Bankruptcy Restriction Orders can be imposed on those considered to have been dishonest, reckless or blameworthy. In these extreme cases, the orders can last for up to fifteen years and prevent people from getting credit of more than £500 without disclosing their status, acting as a director of a company, and trading under different names. Breaching such an order is a criminal offence.

It's worth noting that the above legal procedures are applicable in England, Wales and Northern Ireland only. There are similar mechanisms available in Scotland but the process is different. The equivalent of an IVA is known as a Trust Deed and bankruptcy is called Sequestration. The Statutes in countries outside of the United Kingdom may be different, so check this out with your local authorities.

7

Section

Key Practical Steps to Debt-Freedom

Frankly speaking, there are only two ways to get out of debt.
1. Spend less.
2. Earn More.

It sounds so simple and yet anyone struggling to get out of debt will know that it's easier said than done. It requires patience, determination and above all, an action plan. And as we like to say a journey of a thousand miles begins with a single step so follow as many of these tips as you can and start your long walk to Debt Freedom Day:

1. Start by working out how much you owe

Do the sums. You need to know precisely how much in debt you are and who you owe money to. Make a particular note of any priority debts as these are the most important ones.

<u>How To Prioritise Debts</u>

Anyone being chased by creditors will know that it's not much fun. There's also the temptation to rob Peter to pay Paul especially if Paul's shouting loudly enough for his money!

However, be careful that you don't fall into the trap of paying the wrong bills if you haven't got enough money to spread amongst all your creditors. Some of them have

more power than others and they're the ones you need to pay attention to first because the consequences of not paying them can be severe.
Priority debts include:

1. Non payment of rent - the landlord can get a court order to evict you;
2. Failing to keep up mortgage repayments - the lender can ask the court to make an order to evict you and sell your home;
3. Failing to pay fuel bills - your gas or electricity can be cut off;
4. Failing to pay the phone bill - the phone can be cut off;
5. Non-payment of Council Tax - you can be sent to prison;
6. Non-payment of Income Tax - the Tax Authorities can take bankruptcy proceedings;
7. Non-payment of court fines - you can be sent to prison.

The golden rule is never to ignore priority debts. Any available money should always be used to pay these first before paying your secondary creditors. Unsecured loans, credit cards, hire purchase agreements, store cards, catalogues and mail order are all examples of secondary creditors' bills which should be further down your payment list.

2. Find out what you spend your money on

If you're not sure where your money is going every month, then find out! Just for a month, make a written note of every single penny you spend. It's a bore but you really need to know what you're spending it on so you know which areas you can cut back on.

Find Out Where Your Money Goes

Unless you've always been a whiz with money, you've probably been there at some point. It's a few days until pay-day, you're living off the leftovers in the fridge and writing cheques that you pray won't be cashed until after you've been paid. Where on earth did your salary go?

If you think it's time to find out, then, just for a month, make a written note of everything you spend. If you're handy with a spreadsheet, all the better.

It's an absolute pain having to write down every single penny you spend on a day-to-day basis and it may seem a bit pointless when it's only 50p for a newspaper. But that's the whole point of the exercise!

You'll probably be surprised to find that you spend a fair bit on the small things. Sandwiches and Starbucks coffee, spur-of-the-moment pub lunches, impulse buys and frequent trips to the corner shop for drinks and nibbles on the way home from work – it all mounts up.

One girl I know was horrified to find she'd spent just over £76 on such things in the space of a week. And yet she was struggling to find the £150 a month she needed to pay off a £3,000 loan! If you're struggling too then start with the spending diary.

3. Work out a budget

Write down all your essential expenditure mortgage/rent, Council Tax, utility and food bills. And by 'essential', I mean the bills that absolutely have to be paid every month if you're not to be cold, homeless etc. You need to know how much you have left over to put towards the debts.

4. Get hold of your credit file

Before you start shopping around for better deals you should take a look at your credit file to see whether it looks good or not. This is because you can damage your credit rating if you're not careful.

5. Contact your creditors

You only need to do this if you are in real financial difficulty. Most lenders would rather work out a repayment plan that you can handle, which could include reducing the interest rate you're paying, than bring in an expensive debt collector. So call them, tell them you have a plan of action - and that you need their help to enable you to pay them back in full. If you can't face it, you can get free help via debts counselling charities in your local jurisdictions.

6. Shop around for better deals

This is where you start to try and free up your money so you have more to chuck at your debts. Are you paying too much for your household bills? Can you get a cheaper mortgage? Insurance? What about your utility bills? Check to see if there are cheaper gas or electricity suppliers in your area using the internet.

7. Make your debts cheaper

Shift your credit card debts to a card offering an introductory 0% interest rate (if you can still find it) for balance transfers. Some balance transfer cards will even let you transfer an overdraft - but if you can't find one, consider moving your current account to a different bank which charges less. The more you can save paying interest the more it'll free up money to throw at the debt itself.

8. Snowball your debts

This involves throwing as much money as you can at the most expensive debts first - you want to get shot of high-interest rate debts as quickly as possible. Snowballing was explained earlier in detail.

9. Use your savings to pay off debt.

Debts usually cost you far more in interest than you gain on your savings so if it makes sense to do so use your savings to prune the debts.

10. Get cheaper phone bills

If you tend to use your landline a great deal, you can do it cheaply by signing up to various services available. Search the internet for options.

11. Cut the cost of your mobile phone bills

Mobile phones seem to be considered an essential these days although somehow we all seemed to manage perfectly well without one before they were invented. If you can't do without yours then at least pay less for the cost of your calls.

12. Look for a better internet deal

You can get broadband deals for as little as £15 a month and dial-up is even cheaper.

13. Cancel your gym membership

If you don't use your gym membership much, this is one expense you can cut.

14. Reduce your grocery bill

You can't stop eating but you can stop buying ready-made meals and there's no rule that says you have to have meat *every* day of the week. Another tip is to make sure you don't go shopping on an empty stomach - being hungry while in a supermarket always makes you buy more.

15. Cut out the takeaways

It's all too easy to nip off to the takeaway when you're hungry and you can't face the idea of cooking but try and halve the number of times you indulge in on. Instead, when you do cook, make double quantities of meals that you can freeze so that you can draw on those when you're feeling too tired to cook.

16. Save money on petrol

It's not always possible to walk or cycle everywhere and for many people cars are essential. So use the various web tools and sites to search for cheaper petrol stations in your communities. Every little helps.

Now, to save money on fuel:

1. In the UK, try Findcheappetrol.com website as well as other similar comparison sites?
2. Ensure that your car is regularly serviced and check your tyre pressures regularly. Under-inflated tyres can cost you eight per cent more in fuel and will wear out more quickly, too.
3. Turning off air conditioning and heated rear windows when not required can save a further ten per cent in fuel costs.
4. Remove that roof rack if you don't need it; a fully loaded roof rack can add 30 per cent to fuel consumption.
5. Drive smoothly and consistently. Avoiding harsh acceleration and braking can save you ten per cent in fuel costs (and prevents premature wear and tear).

A third of all car journeys are less than two miles if you can why not walk or cycle? You'll save money and get fitter too. Or car share for that journey to work or the school run. And if you only need a car occasionally, why not see if there is a Car Club in your area?

17. Make your own sandwiches

People spend an extraordinary amount of money on buying sandwiches for lunch when they could easily make one for far less. If you're spending a fiver a day on a sandwich, a can of coke and a packet of crisps, then you're parting with at least £100 a month. Make your own.

18. Stop buying newspapers

Most daily newspapers are available online and, for the most part, you can read them for free. Besides think of all those trees!

19. De-clutter the house and sell the stuff

Remember that one person's trash is another's treasure so just because you don't like something doesn't mean someone else won't. Car boot fairs are wonderful places to get shot of your junk - and make some money while you're at it.

8 Section

25 Quick Money-Saving Tips

Do you feel like giving your finances a short, sharp shock? Is money tight, but you still fancy a summer holiday? Then read on, because these tips could save you thousands of pounds every year. Some of these are repeats from previous sections; but I am presenting it in this section from a potential savings viewpoint. So this summarises other tips we have discussed so far.

1. Take in a lodger

The government allows you to rent out a room in your home and earn up to £4,250 a year without paying tax. To find out how to earn over £80 a week, check out the website of HM Revenue and Customs.

Potential annual saving: up to £4,250 extra tax-free income

2. Buy cheaper insurance and investments

Shop around for all types of insurance, including home, life, health, home, motor, travel or pet cover. Do the same when buying investment, pension and protection plans, because the commissions paid to middlemen by these products can be huge.

Potential annual saving: thousands of pounds over the coming years

3. Give up smoking

Given the price of Cigarettes these days, a 20-a-day habit costs roughly £1,752 a year. Visit www.nosmokingday.org.uk for help and advice on ditching the dreaded weed. As a believer, you should not be smoking in the first place, so seek God's help to stop now.

Potential annual saving: £1,752 for a 20-a-day habit

4. Switch your mortgage

If you can in the current economic climate; switch your home loan without paying a hefty penalty, demand a better deal from your lender. If it refuses to play ball, check the Best Buys in the weekend papers, *Teletext* or online. After you've done your homework, visit a good mortgage broker.

Potential annual saving: £1,200 (based on securing 2% off an interest-only mortgage of £60,000)

5. Cut down on takeaways

Two family takeaways per week at £20 each equals £2,080 a year, which could pay for a foreign holiday. Just one more night in the kitchen per week could save you over a grand a year!

Potential annual saving: £1,040 a year

6. Take your own lunch to work

It's easy to spend £5 a day on sandwiches, snacks and drinks, which comes to £1,200 a year, assuming 240 working days. It's easy to make a tasty lunch for a pound a day.

Potential annual saving: £960 a year

7. Cut back on your satellite package

A premium satellite package can cost as much as £50 a month. Do you *really* need all those extra film and sports channels? You could save £25 a month by switching to a basic bundle of channels.

Potential annual saving: £300 a year

8. Cancel your gym membership

Gym fees vary, but typically are in the region of £50 a month. Your local council-run pool will be much cheaper if you pay as you go.

Potential annual saving: £300 (assuming you halve your fitness spending)

9. Pay by Direct Debit for discounts

Bank clearing house BACS reckons that a typical consumer can save £169 a year by paying bills by Direct Debit. Also, paying by Direct Debit usually means better deals on loans, mortgages and so on.

Potential annual saving: £169

10. Switch gas and electricity suppliers

If you've not done this yet, you've missed out on big savings! Even if you have switched before, it's worth looking for a better deal. Pay by direct debit for the best discounts, and note that 'dual fuel' offers aren't always cheapest! Learn more by visiting uSwitch in the UK and other portals also exist.

Potential annual saving: £150

11. Read a newspaper for free

Most newspapers are available online, so why not read them for nothing? Alternatively, keep up to date with BBC News Online or Sky News. Take a book if you need something to read while commuting. As a special treat, you could treat yourself to your favourite Sunday newspaper as a reward for being frugal!

Potential annual saving: £100-£250

12. Switch your Internet connection

Changing ISP (Internet Service Provider) could save you a tidy sum, whether you have a broadband or dial-up connection. For broadband, check out the internet for all types of ISP

Potential annual saving: £100+

13. Switch your bank account

Most traditional bank accounts pay puny rates of interest when you're in credit, and charge inflated interest rates on overdrafts.

Rule One: DON'T be afraid to switch!

In March 2006, a revised UK Banking Code was introduced, which included new rules designed to make it easier to switch current accounts:

- When you decide to switch, your existing bank must provide your new bank with a list of all your direct debits and standing orders within three working days.
- Your new account must be up and running within ten working days of your application being approved.
- If either bank makes mistakes during the switch, you won't be liable for any charges caused by these slip-ups.

Rule Two: Decide what you want before you buy!

Your personal Best Buy will depend on how you use your account:

> If you never go overdrawn, choose an account that pays a high rate of interest on credit balances, without charging any fees for day-to-day banking.
> If you slip overdrawn by a small amount once in a while, look for an account that offer a fee-free (even interest-free) overdraft of, say, £100 or so.
> If you are overdrawn heavily or often, pick an account that charges no or low overdraft arrangement fees, plus low rates of interest on overdrafts.

Rule Three: Do your research!

To track down the top accounts, visit independent financial researchers like Moneyfacts, which has several tables of Best Buys to suit everyone.

Potential annual saving: £100ish

14. Switch your mobile tariff

Visit Switch with Which? In the UK and other web portals to see how much you could save.

Potential annual saving: £80

15. Find a better savings account

Nearly six out of ten adults believe that they are not getting the best interest rate on their savings.

Potential annual saving: £60 more interest (based on an extra 2% for a deposit of £3,000)

16. Switch your home telephone

Most BT (in UK) users should save money by switching tariff or provider.

Potential annual saving: £50+

17. Use less energy

You don't have to be an eco-warrior to use energy more efficiently! Learn how to slash your fuel bills at good websites like, Save Energy and the Energy Saving Trust as well as many others in the UK.

18. Cut down on alcohol

Ten pints of beer a week (that's twenty units of alcohol, just below the recommended limit for men) costs £25 or more - that's £1,300 a year. Halve your consumption and you'll save over £50 a month. As a believer I will admonish you stop drinking all together; especially if you are in debt. This is possible with God's help.

Potential annual saving: £650

19. Get cheaper motoring

It costs around £104 a week to run the typical private car – do you *honestly* need yours? If you do, find cheaper petrol sources.

Potential annual saving: will vary

20. Find cheaper holidays, flights, hotels and hire cars

If you simply *must* have a holiday instead of paying off any pesky debts, check out main travel websites like ebookers, Expedia, Lastminute and Travelocity.

Potential annual saving: will vary

21. Save on groceries

Collect and use all the coupons or vouchers that you can lay your hands on. Some supermarkets will accept their rivals' vouchers in the USA - try it and see! Also, visit good websites to view all special offers from all leading supermarkets.

Potential annual saving: will vary

22. Use price-comparison websites

Smart online shoppers use one of the many comparison websites that will provide excellent information.

Potential annual saving: will vary

23. Subscribe to your favourite magazines

Sign up for annual subscriptions to get magazines delivered to your door at 25% to 75% off high-street prices.

Potential annual saving: will vary

24. Don't buy extended warranties

Extended warranties on electrical goods are often a complete waste of money. That's because they are usually hugely over-priced - yet modern appliances are becoming ever more reliable. You're better off self-insuring (creating a savings pot for emergencies and repairs).

Potential annual saving: will vary

25. Claim all the benefits you can

Visit free benefits-enquiry websites or call the UK Benefit Enquiry Line for more information.

Potential annual saving: will vary

Don't feel you have to follow all of these tips faithfully - just do what works for you!

9

Section

SEEING AND ENJOYING AN OPEN HEAVEN

"The LORD shall open unto thee his good treasure, the heaven to give the rain unto thy land in his season, and to bless all the work of thine hand: and thou shalt lend unto many nations, and thou shalt not borrow" (Deut. 28:12.)

SEEING AND ENJOYING AN OPEN HEAVEN

'Open heaven' is a phrase used to describe the condition of a Believer who is experiencing all of God's spiritual and material blessings - without fail. There are a number of things you can do if you want to start experiencing an 'open heaven' over your life. They are:

1. **Faithfully tithe on your income. (Malachi 3:10-11.)**

   If you honour God by providing for His Kingdom, God promises to honour you by providing for your needs. You can't get a better bargain!

2. **Sow generously into the Ministry of others. (Luke 6:38.)**

   Ask God to show you a Ministry or Minister (who does what you would like to do, or who simply blesses you) and endeavour to support him/her in any way you can.

"Even when I was over Thessalonica you sent help twice. But though I appreciate your gifts, what makes me happiest is the well-earned reward you will have because of your kindness...... the gifts you sent me...... are a sweet smelling sacrifice that pleases God well. [Therefore]...... He will supply all your needs from His riches in Glory......" (Phil. 4:16-19.) Living New Testament.

3. **Watch your attitude and what you say. (1 Pet. 5:8.)**

   Wrong attitudes (of Pride, taking offences, Strife, etc.) destroy the ground under your feet and close the heaven above your head. They open the door for Satan to come in and cheat you out of what rightfully belongs to you.

THE LAWS OF SOWING AND REAPING-THAT PRODUCE A GOOD HARVEST.

"They that sow in tears shall reap in joy" (Psalm 126:5.)

There are certain physical laws of harvest that are duplicated in the financial realm. If we for a moment consider money, time, gifts etc. to be seeds that can be sown into the grounds of Ministries, Ministers, people, projects etc., then we can apply certain agricultural principles and predict the certain financial outcomes.

The principles that work together to produce a bountiful harvest of Gods blessings in your life are:

1. **Try to plant the seed of the thing you expect to harvest.**

   In real life, if you want to reap apples you don't plant banana trees. However, God is sovereign and sees your heart's desire to please Him. Therefore, if you are standing in faith for a car for your business and don't have a car to give, I believe that you can still sow a seed of something else and God (Who alone sees your heart) would honour your act of giving and obedience.

2. **Make sure that you are sowing your seed in good ground.**
   God does not want us to put our money or time where it would be wasted or mismanaged. So check out the work that is being done by the people and places you support.

3. **When you plant your seed, let go of it.**

   In other words, once the seed is out of your hand, believe that the God who gives life to every seed is giving fruit bearing life to your seed. Don't be tempted to engineer your own harvest.

4. **The size of your harvest is determined by the size of your seed.**

   Every farmer determines the quantity of his harvest when he decides how many seeds he is willing to plant and how much land he is willing to till.

5. **You must water your ground regularly.**

   Farmers know that they can't just plant their seeds and return for the harvest a year later. They must continue to cultivate the ground and feed the crops. You create the right atmosphere for your material and spiritual harvest through prayer and intercession for the ministry or minister you are supporting. Also by 'reminding' God of the seed you sowed when you are praying about your need.

6. **You must wait patiently on God to give you the increase – because the harvest is nothing but a Miracle.**

   Too many Christians run off to get a loan to purchase their harvest. If a farmer did that, we would call him dumb. Well, that is Dumb!

7. **You must be prepared to reap your harvest.**

   It's called Faith! You expect it and you get ready for it, because you know that it's got to come. But remember that harvest time is a busy time for the farmer. Very often God gives you your harvest when you choose not to be lazy.

8. **Part of your harvest is for sowing again, and part is for you to enjoy.**
   Never feel guilty or ashamed to enjoy part of your harvest. Also never consume the whole of your harvest. No wise farmer ever does that. Always sow some of it back into good ground.

CONCLUSION

If you do these things conscientiously and faithfully, you can expect to enjoy **many** bountiful harvest of blessings. And your life will be a melody of miracles!

<u>Notes</u>

10 Section

WAIT FOR YOUR HARVEST

If you have been doing what God wants you to do (eg. tithing faithfully, giving cheerfully, etc.) your harvest would come sooner or later. If it appears to be taking a long time, it is probably because:

1. **Satan is fighting tooth and nail to get you to give up.**

   But if you maintain your ground, you will gain something nobody can take away from you.

2. **It is not yet time for your harvest.**

   Some crops reach maturity in a few months, while others take years to do so. So your attitude should be that the longer your harvest takes to mature, the bigger and better it would be.

3. **You are not totally ready for it.**

   You need to be able to handle what God has in store for you or you can easily lose your harvest. So sometimes God delays giving you your requests until He knows you are mature enough to handle it.

4. **You can do without it.**

   Sometimes, God wants you to do without certain things for a while, because he knows how easily they can overwhelm you. At other times, He just wants you to continue to worship Him even when you have a need that is not being met immediately. That is your faith speaking!

5. **It would hinder your growth and sensitivity to God.**

   There are certain prayers that God answers by keeping certain things from you. Not because He wants to, but because you asked Him to. For instance, a sincere prayer of dedication (eg. **'Lord, use me to expand your Kingdom....'**) may mean that God can only answer that prayer by closing the door to your getting another job, if He wants you to be a full-time minister of the Gospel. Although I believe situations like these are rare, you need to be aware of them.

THE CERTAINTY OF YOUR HARVEST

If you don't give up, your harvest will definitely come because:

1. **God will not lie to you.**

He said if you give to others, He would cause men to give greater measures to you. He said if you bring your tithes into His house, he would pour you out an abundant measure. He is dependable and so is His Word.

> **"God is not a man, that he should lie; neither the son of man, that he should repent: hath he said, and shall he not do it? Or hath he spoken, and shall he not make it good?"** (Num. 23:19.)

2. **God's principles always works.**

The law of gravity is a **physical law** that does not fail. The law of sowing and reaping is a **spiritual law** that cannot fail.

> **"For ever, O LORD, thy word is settled in heaven."** (Psalm 119:89.)

11

Section

THE WISDOM OF GIVING

"For God so loved the world, that he gave his only begotten Son, that whosoever believeth in him should not perish, but have everlasting life." (John 3:16.)

QUESTION:

Why does giving to others play such a key role in your move towards financial independence?

ANSWERS:

1. **God commands you to give.**
   Giving is emulating and obeying God.

2. **Giving is God's answer to greed.**
   Giving suffocates the spirit of greed out of your life.

3. **Giving helps you to put temporary things into their rightful place.**
   People who don't learn to release what they have for the benefit of others, place the material factor above the human factor.

4. **Giving transforms you into a channel of blessings.**
   You become the answer to people's prayers.

5. **Giving makes you a partner with God.**
   You share in the responsibility of establishing God's Covenant on the earth – for which there is an eternal reward.

6. **Giving activates the principle of sowing and reaping for you.**

7. **Giving opens the door for God to bless and reward you Himself.**

8. **Giving opens you up to hear clearly from God.**

9. **Giving produces joy in both the giver and the receiver.**

10. **Giving confuses Satan, and stops him in his tracks.**

Can you think of any other reasons?

____

____

God is not interested in propagating greed. Therefore, he is under no obligation to prosper the greedy soul. So determine today to be a giver, and God will anoint you with the **grace of giving.** (2 Cor. 8:1-7.)

12 Section

Spending from God's Pocket

The Pillars and the Practicalities of Covenant of Increase

For if anyone is a hearer of the word and not a doer, he is like a man observing his natural face in a mirror; for he observes himself, goes away, and immediately forgets what kind of man he was. But he who looks into the perfect law of liberty and continues in it, and is not a forgetful hearer but a doer of the work, this one will be blessed in what he does. **James 1:23-25**

The Bible tells me that idle chatter only produces poverty. And most of our Sunday morning services are nothing but pet talks—we have encouraged people to give money so that God would give back to them. Candidly, God is not a counterfeiter. We beguile people and remove from them the culture of labour, investment, and productivity. We say "if you can just give to me by miraculous swing, you would have a break through"—usually it is the man who preaches to you that would have a breakthrough but you would have a break down—God does not work that way!

So, this message is not about any idle talk but rather a constructive deliberation. It is when you have done your work so thoroughly that you begin to shine to the nations

In all labour there is profit, but idle talk leads only to poverty. Pro 14:23.

You will only prosper by the voice of the Spirit and the enabling grace to obey what you have heard the Spirit says to you.

Who are you financially? My understanding of prosperity may be different from yours. **Each time I step into the subject of prosperity, the first name that strikes me is Joseph**. Although he was a teenage boy that was sold into slavery, the Lord was with him and he was a prosperous man in the dungeon (Gen 39:21-23).

So what are the <u>pillars upon which you can build a life of spending and living out of God's pocket.</u>

PILLAR NO 1 – YOU MUST LIVE IN THE PRESENCE OF GOD

But the Lord was with Joseph, and showed him mercy and loving-kindness and gave him favour in the sight of the warden of the prison. And the warden of the prison committed to Joseph's care all the prisoners who were in the prison; and whatsoever was done there, he was in charge of it. The prison warden paid no attention to anything that was in [Joseph's] charge, for the Lord was with him and made whatever he did to prosper. Gen 39:21-23

That is my very foundation for prosperity. Because if the Lord is with you, and you are with the Lord, and you are constantly in dialogue—you are hearing the voice of the Spirit, then you can spend from God's pocket.

It is the presence of God in your life that makes you a prosperous man, not what you have or what you do not have! Joseph eventually became the administrative general in Egypt and a father to Pharaoh in the entire land because of the presence of God in his life. What do you value more?

On the contrary, **In the case of Judas Iscariot in the New Testament, God was with him but he was not with God.** He did wonderful works in the course of the gospel. However his motive for being with Jesus was the money that he could make, to the extend of betraying his master.

I am trying to say to you, except the motive in you changes you can be in church all your life and Christ might not be in you. **If money is your motive, you will do anything to get it—if all you are in church for is to make quick fixes; how to turn things around, receive the anointing, without any formation of Christ on the inside of you, you are disaster, like Judas Iscariot, going somewhere to happen.**

If God does not enter into you, Satan will, because there is no vacuum in nature—greed for gain will take the life of its owner.

If the foundation of your prosperity is not the presence of God, you are disaster going somewhere to happen! A destructive means will never bring a constructive end, because compromise will only lead to captivity—there is a better way to succeed in life—you can win by righteousness. **God's pocket is in His presence.**

PILLAR NO 2 - AVOID LIVING BASED ON THE EXPECTATIONS OF OTHERS

So, when I say who are you financially, I am not trying to look down on you but rather to let you see where you are.

* Who are you comparing yourself with?
* Who are you trying to please and impress?
* Whose clock are you working by?
* Who determines what you do?

There is a steady pattern in God for you to build wealth in such a way that you will be a blessing to humanity, and you will truly serve your God without pressure.

Please, do not fake it till you will make it—just make it. Do not try to impress anyone. **Live your life normally**.

If you cannot afford anything, tell people you cannot! Let those who are running now, run ahead of you. But when the hand of God comes upon you, you will outrun every Ahab and his chariot unto the gate of Jezereel.

Wait for God. Do it little by little—be patient! The husbandman who is waiting for the latter rain must be patient! There is a time for everything. You will get there if you work at it slowly.

I appeal to you by the mercy of God, become real—live a simple life, not a complicated life. **You can never prosper by other people's expectations**—*it is the expectation of the righteous that shall not be cut off, not what other people expect of him.*

Peter did not want Jesus to die on the cross, but if Jesus had listened to him He would not have died on the cross and fulfil His destiny.

Jesus would not have delivered the people if He had waited to fulfil their expectations of Him. In like manner, you cannot fulfil your God-given assignment by the expectations of other people.

There are three levels when you talk of increase of prosperity:

Survival: When you are trying to stay alive yourself. At this time you need to stay focused and consolidate. Do not scatter you seed at this time.

Sustenance: At this time you can help people because you are sustained—you are stable.

Significant: This is when you begin to contribute to the life of others—you begin to live your life for others—you think of them; you carry them. God prospers you because of other people—*"I will bless you; make your name great, and you will become a blessing"* (Gen 12:1-3).

- Are you at peace with money? That is to say, when you hear the word money what happens? If you are not at peace with money, then you are losing your mind—you are under pressure.
- If you loose your job today or something happens to you; do you have enough savings to maintain the same life style without any income for six months? If not, you are living dangerously—you would be submerged by challenges, overwhelmed, and that would eventually produce nothing but depression.

The day that Abraham gave Melchizedek the tithes of all, was the day **he received the revelation that God is the authentic source of that which would not fail or tarnish. When God becomes your source, you are sure and certain! Everyone around you may not agree, but you know whom you have believed.**

PILLAR NO 3 - BE FULLY PERSUADED OF THE FAITHFULNESS OF GOD

LET IT BE KNOWN TO ALL THAT GOD IS YOUR SOURCE.

- How do you become so confident in God to make Him your only source?
-
-

- If all what God wanted to give to Abraham was gold and silver, why did He ask him to come out of his father house, because he already had gold and silver by then?

The reason was because there is more in God than gold and silver. What really impresses me about God is His faithfulness. **Between Gen 12 and 24 is a demonstration of the faithfulness of God. God is faithful!** He is so utterly dependable .You can rely on Him regardless of what is going in any given society.

- It was the faithfulness of God that saw David through all the ordeals he went through.
- The same faithfulness saw Joshua through all his predicaments. Not one word of God's failed—everything He said came to pass (Joshua 24:14, Num 23:19).
- **To enjoy God's faithfulness; you must hate money. Mat 6:24**

God will not show you a dream that does not exist already. When He shows you a dream of what He would do in you life, it simply means He has already done it before the foundation of the world, but he would fulfil it in His own time.

"Blessed is she who believed, for there will be a fulfilment of those things which were told her from the Lord" that is the faithfulness of God! (Luke 1:45).

PILLAR NO 4 - YOU MUST UNDERSTAND THAT GOD IS A GOD OF BOUNDARY.

Let my people go.....that they may serve me.

- The boundary of the abundant life is obedience which leads to Holiness.

PILLAR NO 5 - YOU MUST UNDERSTAND GOD'S PURPOSE FOR WEALTH.

- God will not give you access to His pocket just to sustain yourself.
- God's pocket is accessed so that you can be a blessing.

PILLAR NO 6 - YOU MUST BECOME A CONDUIT /CHANNEL FOR FINANCIAL RELEASE. (Become a Giver)

* Release is a requirement for Increase.

PILLAR NO 7 - YOU MUST KNOW WHO YOU ARE IN HIM, (IDENTITY).

* Sense of Identity creates Authority

HOW DO YOU SPEND FROM GOD'S POCKET

1. Live (Be) in Him - RIGHTEOUSNESS. You cannot get access to His pocket outside of righteousness.

2. Live by Him - FAITH & WALKING IN LOVE

3. Live like Him - Holiness, Character, and Hardworking. No short-cut.

4. Live for Him - Consecration & Obedience WITH Contentment

5. Live with Him - Joint Account with God. Be addicted to giving.

6. Live as Him - Pursue only His Agenda and Priority. *You cannot take from His pocket to spend against His will.*

7. Live through Him - Be Fully processed by Him. *You must attend your own funeral.* You must set self aside.

Financial Independence is a reality.
Acknowledge it, believe it and work towards it.

13 Section

Ten most frequent questions about Biblical View of Borrowing

Borrowing is an ancient concept that is discussed thoroughly in the Bible, as are many other financial principles.

In today's society we are drowning in debt – *both public and private* – and we consider it normal and God-directed to borrow in order to obtain the things we feel are needed. But what does God's Word say about borrowing? Is it permitted? If so, under what conditions can we borrow? Can families function effectively without borrowing?

Over the years, I have witnessed, read of and also been asked many apt questions on borrowing and biblical viewpoint by many believers. Below is a summary of the top ten questions I believe will help. I trust the answers will be useful for your situation.

1. ***What does the Bible say about borrowing?***
   Scripture very clearly says that neither borrowing nor lending is prohibited, but there are firm guidelines. Borrowing is always negative in the Bible because it is not God's best. But if a person does borrow, the Scriptures are very clear that the money borrowed must be paid back.

2. ***Is overdraft protection a good idea?*** Overdraft protection is not a good idea. It encourages people not to keep their current accounts balanced, and it encourages the use of credit when discipline in spending should be used.

3. ***Does the Bible prohibit a Christian from borrowing money from a non-Christian?***
   God's Word simply says that whatever is borrowed must be repaid. It doesn't specify whether a believer should borrow from another believer or from a non-believer. It doesn't make any difference as far as repayment is concerned.

4. ***How can low-income families avoid borrowing?***
   One of the greatest dangers for low-income families is the use of consumer credit. There is only one way for low-income families to avoid becoming overwhelmed with debt: *do not borrow.*

   That means that families have to spend frugally and discipline themselves to stay on strict budgets. For low-income families, it is probably best not to use credit cards.

5. ***Should people borrow to do the work of the Lord?***
   If a person knowingly violates biblical principles, it is wrong, no matter how noble the purpose. It is unlikely that God would direct anyone to violate His Word to accomplish His work.

   Since borrowing is not God's best for His people, why would He endorse borrowing in order for His work to be accomplished?

   Also in all the temple and tabernacle building projects seen in the Bible, no borrowing took place at all.

6. ***Is it all right for businesses to borrow?***
   It is not any more essential for a business to borrow money than for an individual. God's Word does not differentiate between business borrowing and personal borrowing.

   That doesn't mean that a business cannot borrow. It simply means that when a business borrows it assumes a liability and associated risks, and the money has to be paid back as noted on the agreement.

   In essence, it eliminates God's provision for the business and places that provision in the hands of the lenders. So, borrowing for business is not a sin, but it is also not the best God has to offer.

7. ***Is a lease better than a loan?***
   A lease is basically no different than a loan. When you sign a lease, it's a contingent liability and an obligation to pay. But, the economics of a lease are usually worse than a conventional loan and may actually cost more than a loan in the long run.

8. ***Should home mortgages be refinanced if you can get a better interest rate?***
   If you plan to stay in the home for five years or longer, can lower your fixed interest rate by 2 percent or more than your existing rate, and you do not have to roll the refinancing and associated fees into the new loan, you might want to consider refinancing.

   However, if with your lower monthly payment you cannot pay off the refinancing and associated fees within three years, you might want to rethink your decision to refinance.

9. ***Should I borrow on the equity in my home in order to invest?***
   No matter where funds are invested, they can be lost if there is an economic downturn. But the debt on the house will continue regardless of economic conditions.

   The goal of every homeowner is to have a debt-free home, but not to have a debt-free home so that it can be used as collateral to borrow against. Borrowing against equity in your home is some of the worst financial advice that can be given, regardless of why the equity is borrowed.

10. ***Is it wise to get a consolidation loan?***
    Consolidation loans are tempting because creditors can be paid off and you only have one monthly payment, rather than several. The problem is that a consolidation loan may treat the symptoms for a while, but unless a disciplined and diligent lifestyle is adopted even greater bondage can be created, because past habits have not been corrected.

    Consolidation loans should never be the first step in resolving a debt problem; budgeting and discipline should be.

Conclusion

Although borrowing is not forbidden in God's Word, it is not encouraged, because it is not God's best for His people. His desire is for us to rely on His provision for our needs, not to rely on lenders for that provision. God bless you.

ANNEX 1

Basic Financial Responsibility Test

How good are you with money? Do you spend lavishly on yourself or spouse or do you hoard for a rainy day? Try this fun test below and find out how impulsive you are. But you must be sincere and honest with your answers, if you are to find out the truth about your financial responsibility. **Couples undertaking this test will discover whether they are financially compatible with their partner.**

Please answer honestly based on your present circumstances only, as a false answer will give you a false analysis. There is no right or wrong answer. Put a dash across the answer of your choice like this (≠). Look at the answer page for an interpretation of your position. Good luck.

1. You've inherited £5,000. Would you
A. Book an around-the-world ticket or holiday
B. Invest it in an ISA/shares or savings account
C. Spend it on a permanent fixture for the house

2. If you really wanted something you couldn't afford, would you
A. Wait until you'd saved the money
B. Buy it on hire purchase at zero per cent finance
C. Put it on a credit card

3. If a close family member desperately needed £3,000 would you
A. Give it without hesitation
B. Want to know when it was going to be repaid
C. Avoid lending any money if possible

4. When you go to the supermarket, do you
A. Have a list that you stick to
B. Buy whatever you fancy
C. Buy a few treats but keep an eye on the cost

5. How often are you overdrawn?
A. Seldom
B. Never
C. Always

6. When the credit card bill comes in, do you
A. Pay off the full balance immediately
B. Pay off the minimum only
C. Pay off what you can

7. What are you doing about money and your future?
A. I don't really think about the future - it'll look after itself

B. I'm already saving for my retirement - I don't want to be poor in my old age
C. I'm not doing anything at the moment but know I should start planning

8. What would you spend on an average night out?
A. £0 - 25
B. £25 - 50
C. £50 +

9. How old were you when you had your first savings account?
A. In childhood
B. 18 - 25
C. Over 25

10. When your bank statement arrives, do you
A. Bin it unopened
B. Open it and look at the total balance
C. Check every single entry

NOTES:
Add together the value of each answer you have chosen, (based on the value of each answer as shown in the next page).

Your Total Point Score puts you in one of the three financial groups explained. It also indicates the relationship impact with your partner.

Financial Responsibility Test Results.

QUESTION 1
A = 1
B = 3
C = 2

QUSTION 2
A = 3
B = 2
C = 1

QUESTION 3
A = 1
B = 2
C = 3

QUESTION 4
A = 3
B = 1
C = 2

QUESTION 5
A = 2
B = 3
C = 1

QUESTION 6
A = 3
B = 1
C = 2

QUESTION 7
A = 1
B = 3
C = 2

QUESTION 8
A = 3
B = 2
C = 1

QUESTION 9
A = 3
B = 2
C = 1

QUESTION 10
A = 1
B = 2
C = 3

SCORE ANALYSIS

Cautious but Erratic. (18 -24 points)

That means you know what the right thing to do is financially, but you sometimes let temptation get the better of you and lapse into making an irresponsible financial decision. However you tend to bounce back on to the right track and frequently stick to it for a considerable amount of time. Your credit card balance is probably quite erratic. You admire people in Delayed Gratification category, whereas you empathise with people in Impulsive category.

But don't worry if your partner is not the same financial type. Opposites attract! Many people fall into this category. This is a middle way position, but definitely not a place to dwell for ever. You must move towards delayed gratification for a more stable financial future.

Delayed Gratification and Wise. (25-30 points)

Delayed Gratification types are financially sensible and have the emotional intelligence to wait for things. They are the opposite of 'Impulsive' and staunchly against the school of 'instant gratification'. When making a purchase they nearly always do it after careful consideration and assessment as to whether they 'need' the item as opposed to just 'want' it.

They are heavily critical of people who buy things that they can't afford and least like people in the Impulsive category. This is the best group to be. You are on the road to definite success.

Impulsive & Careless. (10 -17)

In terms of financial decisions that need to be made, Impulsives 'live for the moment'. They believe that life is too short to worry about the ramifications of too many financial commitments. At times their conscience may crucify them, particularly after a busy shopping spree. They are probably already committed to several credit cards as their abiding rule is 'buy today and pay later' or indeed whenever!

Being in the impulsive category is always a warning sign: impulsives run the risk of clashing with those in the Delayed Gratification category in particular. It is dangerous for both partners in a marriage to fall within. This is the worst category you can be financially. You need urgent training in financial management and self control.

ANNEX 2

Financial Control Test

Many people need some professional advise for their financial situation to be sorted out. How do you know if you are such a person? Do you fall into the category of people who can effectively manage their personal situation? If you want to find out whether you are in control of your affairs (in which case you do not really need professional financial planning help), try asking yourself these 11 questions.

1. How much are you **personally worth** right now?

2. Has this figure **increased over and above inflation** since this time last year?

3. How much of your personal worth is **useable** (available to spend or provide an income) and how much is **in use** (e.g. house, car or other asset)?

4. What does your financial worth **need to be** to achieve your objectives?

5. What is your **main investment objective?** Is it obtaining higher income, or more growth, or a combination of the two?

6. If you were to be **disabled today,** what would be the effect on your income and/or assets?

7. If you were **to die today,** would your family be able to continue to live in the way that you would want?

8. How much do you spend, and how much of your spending goes in areas which **increase your wealth?**

9. How will your spending patterns **change when you cease work,** and what income will you require?

10. What is the **worst case outcome** for your current investment strategy?

11. Have you taken advantage of all of your **tax-free allowances?**

If you cannot confidently answer these questions or get the answers worked out on your own, then you may need the help of a financial planning adviser or some other external help.

ANNEX 3

HELP & ADVISE Sources

Noted below are some sources of practical help in debt related matters. The details are correct as at October 2008. These are the organisations to approach in the UK for help and advice:

General

Citizens Advice Bureaux
Check in your local phone directory for your local branch, they really are worth a visit.

Consumers Association
The Consumers Association produces the following publications relating to money. They are available from good bookshops or can be ordered by phoning freephone 0800 252 100 (postage and packing is free).

Which? Way to Save and Invest - £14.99
Which? Way to Save Tax - £14.99
The Which? Guide to Shares - £9.99
The Which? Guide to Insurance - £10.99
The Which? Guide to Gambling (covers everything from horse-riding to enterprise investments, premium bonds, the Lottery and futures) - £9.99
Be Your Own Financial Adviser - £9.99
The Which? Guide to Pensions - £9.99
The Which? Guide to Giving and Inheriting - £9.99
Wills and Probate - £10.99
Make Your Own Will (Action Pack) - £10.99

Office of Fair Trading
Has useful information on its Consumer Help web page.
Web site: www.oft.gov.uk

Debt

National Debtline - 0645 500511
This nationwide service offers confidential expert advice over the telephone and a free information pack called Dealing with Your Debts.
The service is free and calls are charged at local rates.
Monday and Thursday 10am - 4pm, Tuesday and Wednesday 10am - 7pm, Friday 10am - 12 noon.

Bankrupt Advisory Service - 01482 633034 / 35
An independent organisation offering advice to anyone with serious bankruptcy or debt problems, including a negotiation service and telephone advice. This is a subscription-based service costing £15 per year and including a book on debt and bankruptcy in the first year, a regular newsletter and unlimited access to the telephone advice line.

Tax Aid - 020 7624 3768
A free independent advisory service for people with tax problems who cannot afford to pay an accountant.
Open between 10 am and 12 noon, Mondays to Thursdays.

Insurance

Association of British Insurers - 020 7600 3333
Advice and factsheets on insurance and insurers.

Financial Plans

Moneyfacts
This financial magazine lists up-to-date rates of interest on savings, investments, mortgages, credit cards and loans. The magazine is only available on subscription for £58.50 including postage, but you can receive a one-off copy for £5.95 over the telephone on 01603 476100 or by writing to Moneyfacts Publications, Moneyfacts House, 66-70 Thorpe Road, Norwich, NR1 1BJ.

Moneyfacts also publish interest rates for credit cards, savings accounts and mortgages on Ceefax pages 252-258 and Skytext pages 250-253.

IFA Promotions - 0117 971 1177
For a list of three independent financial advisers in your area, a general information pack and a coupon for a free first consultation, call the above number. However, the advisers on the list are not endorsed or recommended by IFA Promotions and we would advise seeking a personal recommendation from a friend.

Money Management National Register of Independent Fee-based Advisers
Matrix Data Ltd
Freepost 22 (SW1565)
London W1E 7EZ
020 7734 8334

Institute of Financial Planning
Whitefriars Centre
Lewins Mead
Bristol BS1 2NT
0117 945 2470

Small Businesses

Businesslink - 0345 567 765
Businesslink offers advice to small businesses, including free factsheets on various useful topics (eg writing a business plan). To find your local centre call the above number or visit the Small Business Service, a government agency, at http://www.businessadviceonline.org/

Parenting

The Maternity Allowance
This is an independent national organisation that campaigns for improvements in rights and services for mothers, fathers and babies. It works for better provision before conception, during pregnancy, childbirth and the first year of life. You can call the information line number below for factsheets and advice or write, outlining your exact situation for more specific information.

The Maternity Allowance
45 Beech Street
London EC2P 2LX

Information line: 020 7588 8582

Unemployment Unit and Youthaid
Youthaid publish a detailed booklet called Under 18 and Pregnant. It is available from Central Books:
99 Wallis Road
London E9 5LN
020 8986 4854

UK Parents
UKparents online offer a unique website and online community, specifically for parents and parents- to-be in the UK. They supply up-to-the-minute information, support, advice and friendship, 24 hours a day.
www.ukparents.co.uk

For information by post or phone contact:
196 Portland Road
Jesmond
Newcastle upon Tyne
NE2 1DJ
0870 907 9111

'Baby on a Budget' *by Noelle Walsh.*
Published by Pan, priced £3.99 at all good bookshops. This book is packed with entries on where to buy the best for your child without ever having to pay the full price.

Relationship

Relate
Relate offers confidential relationship counselling to anyone, regardless of marital status, age, race, personal beliefs, sexual orientation or social background. They also offer psychosexual therapy. There are 112 Relate centres in England, Wales and Northern Ireland. Each Relate centre is an independent organisation that is registered as a charity in its own name. All centres are affiliated to National Relate and abide by its standards. To find your nearest centre look in the local phonebook under Relate or Marriage Guidance or consult their website at www.relate.org.uk

Students

Credit Action Student Helpline
Tel: 0800 591084 (freephone)

Student Loan Company
Tel: 0800 405010 (freephone)

Elderly

Age Concern England
For details of local branches and fact-sheets on financial issues relating to older people.
1268 London Road
London SW16 4ER
Tel: 020 8679 8000
Website: www.ace.org.uk

Help the Aged Advice Lines
Senior-Line for free welfare rights advice on 0808 800 6565. Retirement and Property service 0800 413 180
Accident Cashplan 0800 0962541
Care Fees advisory service 0500 767 476
Monday - Friday 9am - 4pm
website: www.helptheaged.org.uk

IFA Care
For details of Independent Financial Advisers who specialise in long-term care arrangements.
Tel: 01299 406040
website: www.ifacare.co.uk

ANNEX 4

NO MORE DEBTS
FAMILY BUDGET WORKSHEET

FOR THE PERIOD OF __________ MONTHS

MONTHS FROM: ________________TO: _________________ YEAR:__________

PROJECTED INCOME

Cash Income:			
Gross Employment Salaries	£ ____________	+	
Net Profit from Small Business	£ ____________	+	
Income from Property Rentals	£ ____________	+	
Income from Fixed Deposits	£ ____________	+	
Debtors Collection	£ ____________	+	
Other Income	£ ____________	+	
	TOTAL INCOME	=£ ____________	**A**
Less Tithe & Cash Gifts	£ ____________	-	**B**
Less Taxes and other Deductions	£ ____________	-	**C**
	NET RESOURCES AVAILABLE:	=£ ____________	**D=A-(B+C)**

PROJECTED EXPENSES

FAMILY EXPENSES			Actual %
Housing (including utility)	£ ____________	+	
Food	£ ____________	+	
Transport (Auto)	£ ____________	+	
Household Goods	£ ____________	+	
Clothing	£ ____________	+	
Education & Entertainment	£ ____________	+	

Loan Payments	£ ____________ +	
Health & Insurance	£ ____________ +	
Other Goods & Services	£ ____________ +	
Other Expenses	£ ____________ +	
TOTAL FAMILY EXPENSE	**=£ ____________**	**E**
SAVINGS FOR CONTINGENCY	**+£ ____________**	**F**
TOTAL EXPENDITURE	**=£ ____________**	**G=E+F**
PROJECTED FAMILY SURPLUS	**£ ____________**	**H=D-G**

P.S. Remember John Wesley's advice on money:

"*Earn all you can; save all you can; give all you can!*"

ANNEX 5

How To Get Out Of Debt - An Illustrated Guide To Debt Reduction

If you want to get out of debt, you need three key things - a plan, some money, and lots of determination. I can't provide you with the money or the determination, but I can give you some ideas for how to create a workable plan.

1. **List your creditors, your current balances and your current interest rates.**
    - If you want to rid yourself of those pesky smaller balances, regardless of interest rates, list your debts smallest balance to largest balance. This method is commonly referred to as the Debt Snowball.
    - If you want to ensure that you will pay the smallest amount of interest, over the course of your debt reduction, list your debts highest interest rate to lowest interest rate. This method is commonly referred to as the Debt Avalanche. (Source: Consumerism Commentary)
    - If you simply have a debt that you want pay off first, regardless of its balance or its interest rate, list it first. Then, list your other debts accordingly.
2. **Make minimum payments to all of you accounts.** For your credit cards, this would be the minimum payment listed on your monthly statement. For your automobile loan, this would be the monthly payment. Make a note of these initial minimum payments.

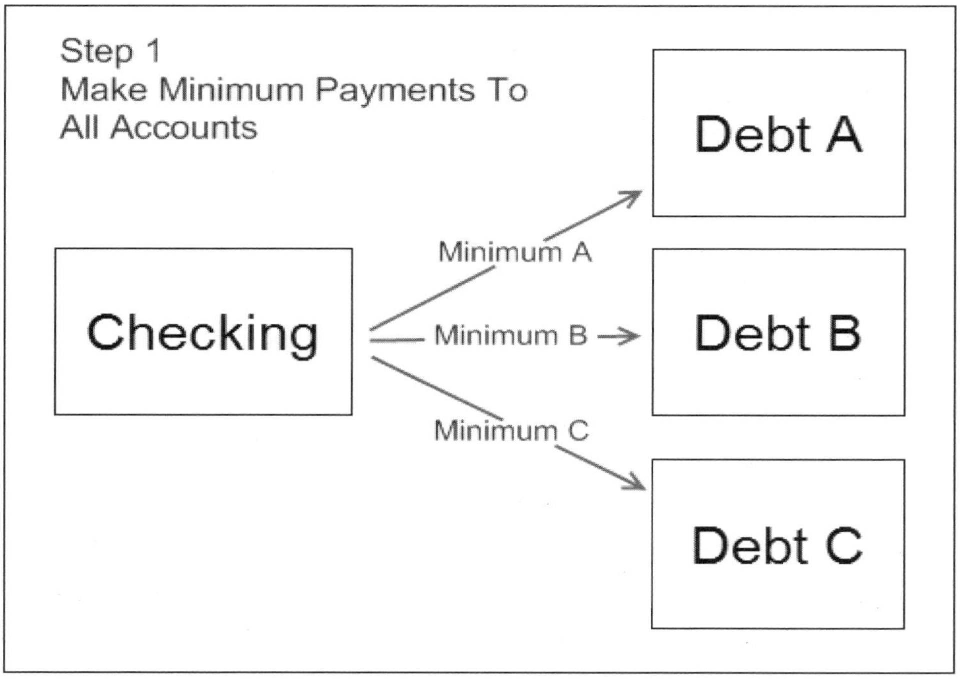

3. **Make an extra payment to the account at the top of your list.** When sending payment, write "apply to principal" on the memo line of your check. Using online bill pay (initiating payments from your checking account to your creditors) is a simple way to send extra payments, without having to deal with envelopes or stamps.

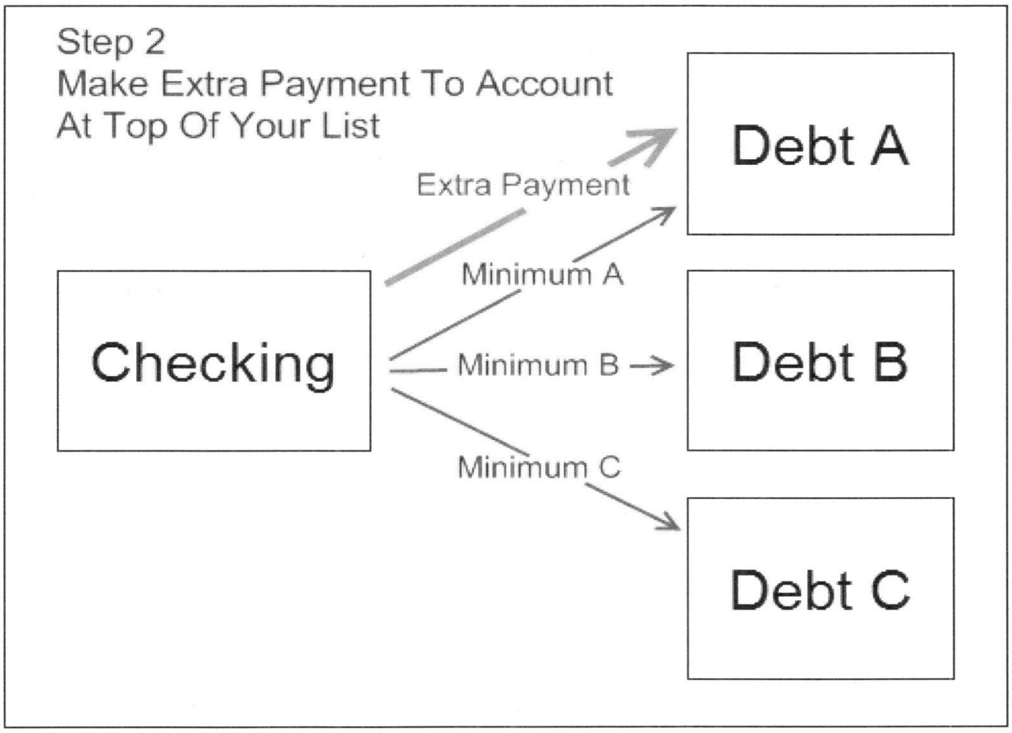

4. **Continue sending minimum payments and your extra payment until the first debt on you list is paid off.** Then, combine your extra payment AND the minimum payment that you were sending to the first account, and send that combined amount to the second account on your list. This is where the snowball / avalanche effect really starts to work. Do not relax. Remember how I mentioned that you needed a plan, money, and determination? This is where the determination really matters. It would be so easy to spend the minimum that you had been spending to the first account, but then you would lose the impact of the snowball. Maintain your intensity and stay focused!

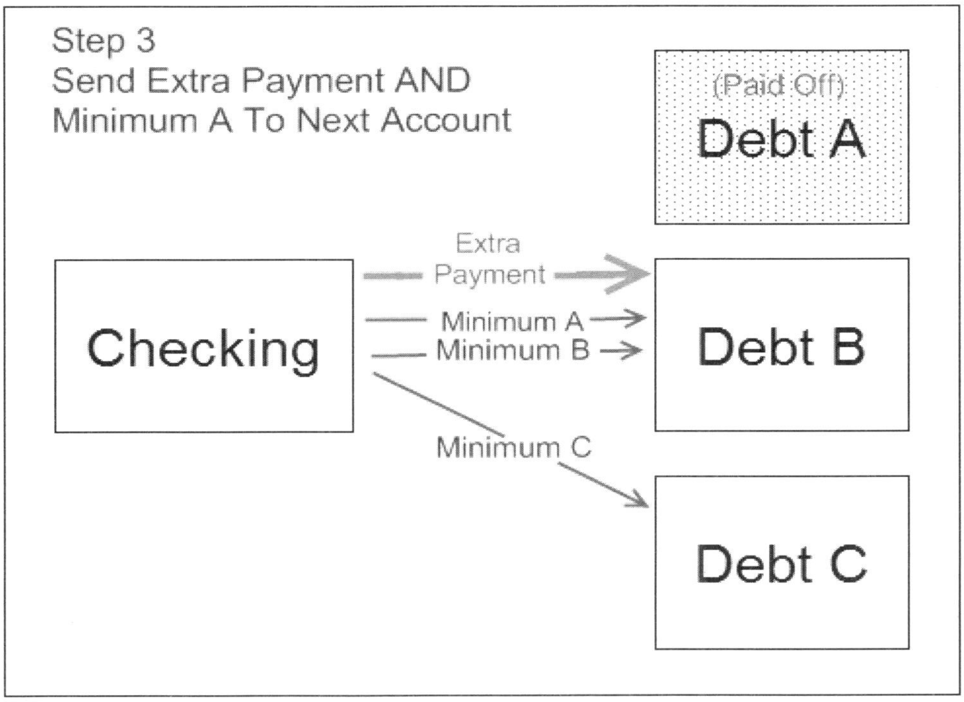

5. **By now, you have this figured out.** Once you pay off the second debt, send the extra payment and the two original minimum payments to the next debt on your list. Continue combining these minimums and extra payments until you are debt free!

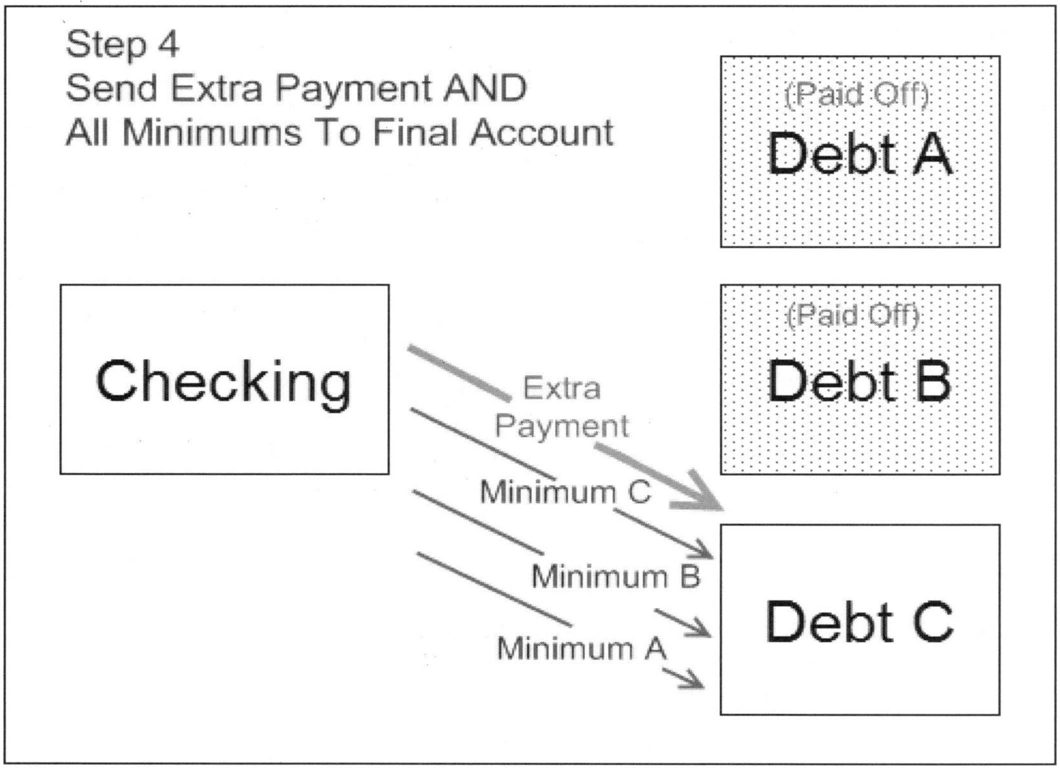

6. **Want to do even more to ramp up your debt reduction?** Don't send one extra payment, send multiple extra payments. Keep your eyes open for ways to reduce your interest rates. Consider calling your credit card companies and asking them to reduce your rates. Carefully consider consolidating credit card debt from higher rate cards to lower rate cards.

Source: http://www.ncnblog.com

Books by Pastor Charles Omole

1. Church, Its Time To Fly -- *Learning To Fly On Eagles Wing.*
2. How To Avoid Getting Hurt In Church -- *13 Steps That Will Protect You And Help Create An Atmosphere For Breakthroughs.*
3. Must I Go To Church -- *8 Reasons Why You Must Attend Church.*
4. Freedom From Condemnation -- *Breaking Free From The Burden And Weight Of Sin.*
5. I Cannot Serve A Big God And Remain Small
6. How To Start Your Own Business – *A Summary Guide*
7. How To Make Godly Decisions
8. How To Avoid Financial Collapse
9. Let Brotherly Love Continue: *An Insight Into Love And Companionship.*
10. Breaking Out Of The Debt Trap
11. Common Causes Of Unanswered Prayer.
12. How To Argue With God And Win -- *Biblical Strategies On Getting God's Attention For All Your Circumstances All Of The Time*
13. Avoiding Power Failure -- *How To Generate Spiritual Power For Daily Success And Victorious Living.*
14. How Long Should I Continue To Pray When I Don't See An Answer?
15. Success Killers: *7 Habits Of Highly Ineffective/Unsuccessful Christians*
16. The Financial Resource Handbook – UK Edition
17. Divine Strategies For Uncommon Breakthroughs.
18. Wrong Thoughts, Wrong Emotions Wrong Living
19. Prosperity Unleashed
20. Secrets Of Biblical Wealth Transfer
21. Journey Into Fulfilment

For more information, contact us at:

Winning Faith Outreach Ministries
Kingdom Prosperity Revival Series
Transition Manor
16 Linden Grove,
Great Linford
Buckinghamshire.
MK14 5HF
Email: admin@charlesomole.org
www.charlesomole.org

Notes

Notes

Notes

Notes